MW01284607

**Other Atomic Drop Press titles by
Will Jacobs & Gerard Jones**

Million Dollar Ideas

My Pal Splendid Man

The Mystery of the Changin' Times

My Tongue Is Quick

The Max Kleinman Reader
(with James W. Zook)

The Beaver Papers

The Beaver Papers 2

The Fall of the Beaver

Will Jacobs & Gerard Jones

 Atomic Drop Press

Copyright © 2014 by Will Jacobs and Gerard Jones
Revised 2018

This book is in no way authorized by NBCUniversal or anyone owning rights in or to the television series *Leave It to Beaver*. No one involved with *Leave It to Beaver*, past or present, is in any way associated with this book. This is purely a work of parody, and the names of real persons and institutions are used solely for the sake of satire. All materials herein ascribed to other authors are in fact parodies written by the authors of this book.

All rights reserved. No part of this book may be reproduced or transmitted in any form or by any means, electronic or mechanical, or by any information storage and retrieval system, without permission in writing from the copyright holders.

ISBN 978-0-9827669-8-9

Published by Atomic Drop Press
www.atomicdroppress.com

*To Agnes Jacobs and Jennie Kajiko,
wives so tolerant that they actually
allowed us to make the time for
this strange labor of love.*

Contents

Foreword

It was the best of times. It was the worst of times. Gasoline was a buck thirty-five, but there was no Google. A decent L. A. bungalow rented for $500, but there were no Starbucks.

(With apologies to Charles Dickens)

Yes, it was a much simpler era—an era when two struggling writers who had taken jobs at the ABC mailroom could simply stumble across a treasure trove of *Leave It to Beaver* scripts and correspondence in a storage closet while digging for a roll of bubble wrap, market the hell out of them, and build careers on that one discovery.

I was there at the beginning. And it sometimes makes me feel like the Pete Best of the group, but I'd much prefer to think of myself as Will Jacobs and Gerard Jones's Boswell, keeping track of their collective and individual antics and exploits.

And I often have to marvel at their astounding run of good luck. Blind, dumb luck. The bastards. Only a few years after that discovery, Will and Gerard found yet another, newer cache of *Beaver* scripts and letters that never made it onto television or into their first book. This time though, the proposed episodes did not fall into their laps, it took work. Will, as a fledgling antiquarian book dealer, and Gerard, just starting out as a writer of pop-culture history, both came to these scripts at an estate sale in tony Altadena. Lady fortune (if not the god of hard work) once again smiled on the duo. I'm so happy. Elated even. Way to go guys.

I'm sure they asked me to write this foreword for the book out of pity. To hell with them. So let's get on with it. Here for the first time are the damned scripts. Enjoy.

I'd wish them luck, but they already seem to be swimming in it.

J. W. Zook
Author of *USA or Bust*

Beaver authorities or Professors of Beaverism frequently introduce a few pardonable touches of hyperbole into their accounts of this rodent. They think nothing of devoting forty or fifty years to the subject; naturally, anything that isn't a Beaver seems all wrong.

—Will Cuppy

Prologue

Today it is common knowledge that when, on May 3, 1963, the executives at ABC Television threatened to cancel America's most beloved family sitcom, *Leave It to Beaver*, the artistic community of the world rose up to save it.

Over the next four months, during what we have now come to think of as the Summer of the Beaver, dozens of scripts for a hoped-for seventh season of the show poured in from writers and filmmakers as diverse as Ernest Hemingway, Ingmar Bergman, Yukio Mishima, and Ray Bradbury. Leading scholars composed scripts in the styles of the great authors of the past and contributed learned tomes arguing for the cultural necessity of keeping the Cleaver clan alive. Painters, sculptors, and musicians, ranging from Salvador Dali to Bob Dylan, sent in ideas for costumes, sets, theme songs, and whatever else they hoped might aid the cause. Words of support came in from President Kennedy, Pope John XXIII, and even, in fatal defiance of his own Central Committee, Nikita Khrushchev.

All summer long, the entire cast and crew of the show camped out on the Gomalco Studios lot, avidly devouring each new script, welcoming such famous guests as Timothy Leary, Frank Sinatra, and Walt Disney, and holding a vigil until ABC's executives could be persuaded (as all assumed they would surely be) to change their minds. Finally, on September 8, 1963, the executives announced that, despite it all, the series would not be renewed; but by then, *Beaver* had inspired a literary and intellectual flowering such as had not been seen since the Italian Renaissance, or at least since the Bengali Renaissance of the late 19th Century.

We were privileged to be able to uncover and retell the full story of the Summer of the Beaver in our book, *The Beaver Papers* (originally published by Crown Publishers in 1983, now available in a 30th Anniversary Edition from Atomic Drop Press). What we were not able to reveal at that time was that the story did not end on that tragic September morning long ago. Legal difficulties required us to withhold the truth for three long decades, but now that some of the principal figures have left this mortal vale, we are finally at liberty to describe the events of what will surely become known as the Fall of the Beaver.

We are currently preparing a full, annotated, multi-volume edition of all the scripts, books, songs, paintings, and other creations of that remarkable time, but until that task is completed we feel we owe the world, at the very least, a brief survey equivalent to the original *Beaver Papers*. We here present twenty-five previously unpublished scripts, summarized with an eye toward preserving, as best as possible, the style of each original author, accompanied by brief notes on the heroic efforts of the cast and producers of *Leave It to Beaver* to save their show.

Let us begin where our first volume left off, in the moments after the executives of the American Broadcasting Company stuck their heads into the Gomalco lot and callously announced, "You can all pack up and go home now. *Leave It to Beaver* has been canceled." A hush fell over the lot. And the cast began to weep.

September 8, 1963

The sounds of weeping filled the air over Gomalco. Hugh Beaumont, who played Ward Cleaver on the show, looked over the lot that had been the site of so many hopes throughout the summer and turned his face away from the others so that they could not see his tears. Jerry Mathers, the Beaver himself, tried to take it like a man, but as soon as his eyes met the tear-filled gaze of Barbara Billingsley, the actress who had immortalized the role of his mother, June Cleaver, he too broke down.

As afternoon turned to dusk, the sounds of grief gave way to a mournful silence. All the residents of that once-boisterous camp turned to taking down their tents, rolling up their sleeping bags, and packing up their cooking and sporting equipment. But then one voice shattered the silence. "Are we gonna let this beat us?" it exhorted. "Are we gonna let everything that Beaver means to the world die just because a few old guys in suits tell us to get lost?"

The voice belonged to Tony Dow, who played Wally, the Cleavers' confident and athletic older son. He had leaped atop one of the ping pong tables and poised there glaring challengingly at the assembled group. Shaking his fist, he said, "So what if ABC canceled us? There's still

CBS and NBC!" When Jerry Mathers pointed out that ABC had only begun broadcasting the show after CBS had canceled it five years before, Tony shook his fist again and said, "So there's still NBC, isn't there?"

Hugh Beaumont had been looking on worriedly. "Now Tony," he called, "there's no sense in getting yourself worked up." But for once, Tony would not listen to his surrogate father. Leaping off the table, he strode to the stack of scripts that had been pouring in since May and started searching through them frantically. "I'm going to take the best script we've got straight to NBC—and when they see it, you can bet they'll see what those lunkheads at ABC can't!" Soon enough he found the script he considered the best of all, which happened to be one that focused almost entirely on Wally. Written by James Leo Herlihy, it told a powerful tale of friendship, coconuts, and closeted homoeroticism.

Midnight Beaver

James Leo Herlihy

In the cowboy boots that Aunt Martha sent him for Christmas, Wally Cleaver is nearly five foot ten and life is different. For a year he's been wrestling with what he thought would be the biggest decision of his life, whether to go to State or Valley, but looking at himself in the mirror he knows that State and Valley combined don't have room in them for a Wally Cleaver.

Lumpy Rutherford has told him that men in the city are just faggots mostly, and so the rich city women have to pay for what they want. Wally is unclear on what a faggot is, but he's fairly sure he isn't one, especially in his tall boots, Stetson hat, western shirt, and fringed letterman sweater, and so the city women will pay plenty if he gives them what they want.

The man at the bus station just looks at him blankly when he says, "I want a ticket to the city." Wally is unsure of what cities Mayfield might be near, and so he tells the man the name of the one place he knows of for sure, which is Bell Port, and an hour later he's striding through the streets of the town wondering if Bell Port is big enough to hold a Wally Cleaver. He's a beautiful animal, this Wally Cleaver, with his pug nose and curly hair and what all the Mayfield High girls call dreamy eyes. But he's not hunting for high school girls now.

"Beg pardon, ma'am," he drawls to a very fat woman with a very small poodle. "I'm new in town and looking for a lady who'll pay for what she wants." The woman laughs in his face, and Wally blushes crimson.

At a soda fountain he knocks back shots of chocolate malted, chasing them down with root beer. Then he hears an annoying voice at his elbow. "Where'd you get that shirt, Elwood? Your Aunt Martha?"

"Eddie!" Wally says. "What in heck are you doing in Bell Port?" Eddie tells him how he got tired of the small time in Mayfield and headed where an operator could make some real money. "O' course, this dump's just a stepping stone. I'm heading for Florida, where a man can live on coconuts and sunshine and not break his ass for nothin'." Wally isn't clear where Florida is, but he asks, "And have they got women there who'll pay plenty for what they want?" Eddie looks at Wally with a new respect. "Say, Loverboy, you're not as square as you look. You're a hustler!" "Hey, I may dress like a cowboy," Wally says indignantly, "but I never stole a head of cattle in my life!"

Just then they're interrupted by two young men with plucked eyebrows and menacing stares. "Didn't expect to see you come back here, Creepo." "My name is not Creepo!" Eddie screams. "My name is Edward Clark Haskell!" But he hurries away, and as Wally follows he notices that Eddie is limping badly and launching into a sickening wet cough. "Geez, Eddie," he says, "since when are you a tubercular cripple?" "I'm not a cripple, I'm a gimp! And this cough's nothin' a trip to Florida won't fix!"

He leads Wally into the condemned building where he's been holing up. Night falls and the cruel cold stabs through Wally like no cold he's ever felt. With a pang of longing he remembers Mayfield and its lack of weather. Eddie, downing cough syrup like it was liquor, shares his street smarts. "These rich suburban chicks can't be cruisin' Bell Port Square looking at the merchandise if they want to be able to show their faces at the next PTA meeting. You follow me, Einstein? You need a middleman, an agent, a representative."

"Gee, I don't know, Eddie," Wally says. "This sounds like one of those nutty schemes of yours that get me in trouble. Like that time Dad tried to teach me about the stock market and you talked me into investing in that rocket factory." Eddie snorts derisively and starts telling him how he can spot a woman who wants a cowboy in her bed. Wally snorts in laughter. "In her *bed*? Why in heck would she want me there?"

Eddie yells, "You got a tin ass, Cornelius? What do you *think* you'll be doing when chicks pay you for what they want?" Wally shrugs. "Shucks, I don't know. All those things women want. Mowing their lawns, washing their cars, taking out their trash."

Eddie goes into a hideous coughing fit. His teeth chatter and he sweats a river. Wally wraps him in his own fringed sweater and heats cough syrup over Sterno, but it's clear that Eddie can't last much longer. He croaks one word. "Florida."

Knowing he has no choice, Wally takes to the midnight streets, standing on one corner after another until an effeminate older man catches his eye. "Evening, son. Has anyone ever told you that you have dreamy eyes?" Wally says, "I need money, mister. I'll do anything to get it. Anything."

An hour later Wally has finished scraping down the man's backyard grill and the man has given him ten dollars and a St. Christopher medal. He drags Eddie to the station and onto a bus. After a while, Eddie pees in his pants and says, "Sorry, Clyde, but I'm never gonna make it all the way to Florida." "That's okay," Wally says. "The bus driver doesn't know where Florida is anyway." Before Eddie can answer, they pull into the warmth of the Mayfield station.

Tag: Wally is filling out his application to State when he notices Beaver preening in the mirror. In the cowboy boots that Aunt Martha sent him for Christmas, he's nearly five foot four and thinks life is different. "Cut it out, Beav. You'll never make it as a male hustler." "Oh yeah?" Beaver sneers. "Now that Creepo's leg is all better, he says he's gonna set me up with every pansy in Florida!" "Aw, come off it!" Wally laughs. "What do you know about gardening?" He throws a pillow that knocks Beaver's Stetson clean off his head.

September 8-9, 1963

The Herlihy script in hand, Tony ran to the nearby pile of rejected props, pulled out the fringed letterman sweater that had been crafted for that very episode in the hopeful days of early summer, and made for the door. Hugh Beaumont tried to intercept him, but the youngster eluded him, thanks to all the track and field practice that he engaged in as part of his rigorous training to bring verisimilitude to Wally Cleaver.

Hugh told the group, "I'm afraid Tony's only setting himself up for more disappointment. I wish I'd been able to have a man-to-man talk with him about accepting reality. I wouldn't feel right about leaving until I know he's back safely, so I'll wait. But the rest of you can go on packing if you want." Most of the others went back to their melancholy work, but then Barbara Billingsley announced that if she left she'd only be worrying about Tony, too. Ken Osmond, who played Wally's best friend Eddie Haskell, echoed her sentiments. By nightfall, only a few crew members had left the encampment.

As it turned out, the impulsive Tony had decided to camp at NBC's Burbank studio until he got an audience with the executives, and by the next morning he had not returned. Everyone awoke to discover not only his absence, but that the morning papers all carried the news that *Leave It to Beaver* was no more. "I had woken up in my tent half-believing it was all a terrible dream," said Madge Blake, who portrayed the mother of Beaver's best friend Larry. "When I saw it right there in the headlines, I started crying all over again."

Then the mail delivery brought its usual spate of submissions from the literary and artistic worlds, and for a brief shining moment many others wondered if it had all been a bad dream, too. But when Burt Mustin, the character actor who gave life to old Gus the Fireman, pointed out that they all must have been mailed before word of the series's cancellation had broken, grim reality returned. Among the scripts were Carson McCullers's *The Beaver Is a Lonely Hunter*, Ralph Ellison's *Invisible Beaver*, and Richard Brautigan's *Trout Fishing in Mayfield.* Most of the gang felt too heavy-hearted even to glance at them, but Jerry Mathers, to take his mind off the agonizing wait, opened a package that contained a script from fledgling New Journalist Tom Wolfe.

The Electric Kool-Aid Kleaver Picnic

Tom Wolfe

So the door to this impossibly 100 percent perfect Middle Class house opens and out glides this cool chick in chiffon and pearls, a picnic basket rocking so daintily and weightlessly over her arm that you'd never think it could contain enough food to feed a sparrow, let alone a family of four. She looks over her shoulder and here comes a cat that you can tell right off is as mad as a hatter, wearing this hip golf-sweater-and-slacks ensemble and the...shoes—how they shine!—and cradling a pint-sized cooler. He does the same twist-and-gape and out bounds this teenager in checked shirt and these crazy white chinos that proclaim MOD FREAK as if written in Day-Glo letters, toting a towel and looking extraordinarily like Bucky Barnes, if you remember him from the comics. He looks over his shoulder too, and out flies the coolest, gawkiest, biggest-headed kid you ever saw, leaping a hedge, diving into that Bauhaus-sleek Plymouth Fury, and then, as it backs right at you, beaming through the back window like a buck-toothed Cheshire Cat on the dread LSD!

Beautiful...the current fantasy...the Merry Kleavers out for a picnic!

The Plymouth blazing through a Mondrian painting of white sidewalks and green lawns (Huxley's reducing valve irrigating the suburban dream!), everywhere crazy-grinning dads zipping around with clippers, Apollonian lads pushing lawn mowers. And here come the moms, in cocktail dresses and high heels, bearing trays laden with these beaded pitchers full of what you know must be Kool-Aid. And now the Kleavers hit the shopping district. The Mayfield Bank! The Mayfield Drug Store! The Mayfield Church! And here's the Mayfield Malt Shoppe with its gleaming Formica counter, serving pure vanilla teens. Business cats walking down the street in matching suits and a slick mom pushing a streamlined baby in a tangerine-flake stroller. Man, it's so perfectly American Small Town that it just has to be a put-on! And look, there's the Mayfield Bookstore. For a minute you expect to see Kerouac's *On the Road* and the *Tibetan Book of the Dead* and I Ching yarrow stalks displayed in the window…but you don't! And that's just it…you don't! It's all so studiedly unhip that it's the hippest place on earth!

Haul ass, and there they are, past the Mayfield city limits. But where is this Mayfield? California? Ohio? Nobody knows. You look for clues: there's Friend's Lake, Camelback Cutoff, Crystal Falls, Bell Port. And that's it. You know it's not the South, because the skin tones here are as monochrome as a Barnett Newman painting (and they still talk about that wedding reception where they first heard of the Langleys' Negro maid). But do they care where they are? Why would they?!

Ward, the holy primitive, the *natural*, sits hunched over the wheel in a kind of kinetic trance. June, the eternal beatific pioneer wife, pats his arm and turns in her seat to smile that Mother Earth smile at the boys. And the boys...the BOYS! How to tell it...the current fantasy? Anticipation? Hell no! It's a NOW TRIP. It's a risk-all balls-out plunge into the country, whether it appears on any map or not. That's the way it is in the careening, crazy-dreaming rhythm of the car, everything becoming allegorical, understood only deep in the KLEAVER MIND. And the meaning is this: You're either on the picnic...or you're off the picnic.

The leaves are changing color, a cataclysmic clash of seasons, Dr. Strange vs. Baron Mordo! Anyway, that's the way the kid describes it, the cool kid with the big head, and the others get it right away. That's the way it is with the Merry Kleavers. They pick up on the most banal comments as if they were metaphors for life, all their lives becoming more fabulous every minute like the most fabulous TV show. It's phony, goddamn it...but...after a while it just gets to you, like if their lives were syndicated you'd make time every day out of your own life to tune in on the fruits of love and euphoria and cornball humor.

The cool kid with the big head says, "Hey, Dad. Are we almost there?"

And the dad says, "Just a little further, Beav."

Further! But exactly! It's what Joachim Wach called "the experience of the holy." What George Webber called the "possession of the deity." What Eddie Haskell, with that zoned-out stoned-out madcap simplicity, would term "crazy, Lionel!" But better to back off. To define it is to limit it. FURTHER.

That's all. Period.

Tag: Beaver peels back the covers from his bed and says, "Gee, Wally. Until our picnic today I never realized what a hip family we are." Wally says, "Heck yeah we're hip, Beav. Do you think a hip young representative of the New Journalism with a Ph.D. from Yale and a wild Edwardian jacket would hang out with us all day if we weren't?" Wally flips off the light, but the room remains crazily lit, as if Salvador Dali, spinning like a dervish, had daubed the air itself with mad streaks of Day-Glo paint.

September 9-10, 1963

Thrilled to discover that *Leave It to Beaver* had somehow become hip, Jerry Mathers began excitedly telling whoever would listen that the executives at NBC would surely have to see the light. While all the other young actors agreed enthusiastically that a show as hip as theirs could never be canceled, the adult members of the cast and crew tried to protect them from a painful disillusionment. Hugh Beaumont even led Jerry toward the old Cleaver den set, intending to give him a lecture on the importance of curbing one's imagination, but upon discovering that the den had already been converted into a native hut for *McHale's Navy* he forgot what he had intended to say.

Bob Mosher and Joe Connelly, the show's creators, producers, and head writers, felt troubled. As Connelly later recalled, "Me and Bob, we never thought we'd see the Generation Gap afflict our little TV family. But gosh almighty, those were trying times!"

It was little ashen Stanley Fafara, who played Beaver's friend Whitey Whitney, who summed up the cultural divide: "We of the atomic generation understand the ironic self-referentiality of so-called 'camp,' while the older generation is blinded by its pre-war earnestness. In fact, I was just telling my friend Susan Sontag that she should write an essay about it."

Tony Dow called to say that they would have to wait until the next morning for a decision from NBC, and while the older residents bedded down for one last night on the lot, the younger generation stayed up all night, reading through past scripts and looking for evidence that their show was hip.

But late the next morning, Tony returned. Gone was the bounce from his step, gone was the vim and vigor that he'd displayed the day before. No one needed to hear him speak to know that NBC had said no.

Before any of the adults on the lot could finish saying, "I told you so," the teens were insisting that they had to take one more shot, this time at CBS. "Sure," whined Rusty Stevens, who played Beaver's porcine pal Larry Mondello, "when they canceled us five years ago they didn't know we were hip. We didn't even have a jazzy theme song then." Then Frank Bank, who played Wally's obnoxious friend Lumpy Rutherford, announced excitedly that he had heard that CBS was actively looking for a hip new crime show. For a moment the youngsters buzzed with excitement, but when Hugh pointed out that *Leave It to Beaver* had nothing to do with crime, they all fell silent.

But just then the day's mail arrived. Although it included such contributions as Ian Fleming's *Beaverfinger*, Grace Metalious's *Mayfield Place*, and Anita Loos's *Gentlemen Prefer Beavers,* it was another submission that got everyone buzzing again: a script from the criminally overlooked master of crime fiction, Jim Thompson.

The Beaver inside Me

Jim Thompson

(*Beaver narrates.*)

I was walking down the street when I heard him. "Come over here, Beaver!" I recognized the cracked old voice of Gus the Fireman, and for a second I wanted to run. But you know what they say. Never paddle against the current.

Well, sir, I immediately went into my act, fiddling with my cap, making sure my shirt was buttoned to the throat, flashing my buck-toothed grin. An ounce of prevention is worth a pound of cure, I always say. I'd worked dang hard on my perfect-child routine, and I knew there'd be trouble if the old bum had seen through it. As it turned out, though, he just wanted to tell me some of his musty old stories. Gus could lay on the corn as thick as I could. The only difference was, he meant it.

All the way to Miller's Pond I kept glancing over my shoulder. I was nervous as a long-tailed cat in a room full of rocking chairs, but nobody seemed to be paying me any mind. Finally I was off the street and cutting through the trees. I started peeling off my clothes before the water even came into view. When it finally did I broke into a run and dove in. Boy whiz, that water was so cold it dang near froze my sacs off!

When I got used to the cold I just let myself float. I needed to figure out once and for all what the heck I was going to do about Judy Hensler. If only she hadn't loved it when I did those things to her! Just thinking about it I could feel the sickness coming on, and suddenly I was slapping the water for all I was worth, setting up a clamor you could have heard in Bell Port. Well sir, the last thing I wanted was to attract attention, so I grabbed my clothes and dashed behind a tree faster than a greased pig at the rodeo.

When a few minutes went by and nobody showed up to see what the commotion was all about, I started back for the water. But then the sickness came over me full bore. Before I could even think about it I was gnawing on a tree trunk. I don't know how long I went at it. When I came back to my senses I could tell by where the sun sat in the sky that I'd better be getting home, and fast.

But it just plumb wasn't meant to be. Suddenly, out of nowhere, Judy was there. "Oh, Beaver," she sighed. "Don't you want to…gnaw on me again?" And just like that my sacs started giving off that smell, and I knew the jig was up.

Well, sir, as I've often been heard to say, if life gives you lemons, make lemonade. I sunk my fist up to the wrist in her stomach. Then I went to work on her in earnest, and when it was done I dragged her to the pond and threw her in. I dove in after her, and made sure her body was wedged in the dam I'd built the week before. By the time they found the body the bones would be as bare as a fat man's larder.

Tag: When we were brushing our teeth Wally said, "Geez, Beav, are those wood chips in your mouth?" I told him it was chunks of beef jerky, and before he could ask any more questions I went to work on him with a pillow. But good.

September 10-11, 1963

Armed with the Thompson script, Frank and Jerry rattled
off toward CBS Television City in Frank's jalopy. Hugh
looked after them worriedly and swore to remain on the set
until he knew Jerry was back safely. As it turned out, Frank
and Jerry came back only an hour later, but they brought no
relief to those waiting. A junior executive had heard them
out, but no decision would be made until the next day.

Although a few more minor crew people drifted off,
everyone else chose to stay, unwilling to give up on their
last hope. But whereas during the summer every night had
been filled with badminton, folk singing, and marshmallow
roasting, on this night no one found the heart to do anything
but sit by their dimly lit kerosene lamps, alone with their
own private thoughts.

The same gloom hung over the lot the next morning
when the mail arrived. Coincidentally, two proposals came
in from toy makers. The Marx Toy Co. proposed Rock 'Em
Sock 'Em Squirts; the object in this was not, as with the
more famous product that would be derived from it a year
later, for the combatants to knock each other's blocks off,
but to punch each other in the stomach. The other proposal
came from Hasbro, who hoped to test-market its soon-to-

be-released G. I. Joe action figure by first manufacturing one of Beaver Cleaver. Beaver was a particularly attractive model for a launch because the company wouldn't have to invest much in accessories, as Beaver wore essentially the same outfit in every episode. Frank Bank quipped that someone should come out with a line of Silly Putty that came not in a plastic eggshell but rather in plastic models of a beaver's castor sacs.

Some nonfiction tomes also arrived. Among them were Jean Kerr's *Please Don't Eat the Beavers*, J. Edgar Hoover's *Beavers of Deceit*, and John Howard Griffin's *Buck-Toothed Like Me*, in which the author related his experiences traveling the country disguised as Beaver Cleaver. But more significant was the arrival of a script by that maestro of suburban angst, John Updike.

Beaver, Run

John Updike

Ward in the den that's in the house that's in Mayfield that's somewhere, he isn't sure where, brown eyes marked with paler flecks gliding over what he sees without seeing what he sees. Shelves, books. He has a sense, a sense as deep as it is shallow, that something is missing. What's missing he doesn't know, only that he can see its missingness as clearly as the brown wood marked with paler grain, like flecks in eyes, in the empty space on the second shelf from the top.

June opens the door and smiles that the pot roast is ready, but his eyes fix absurdly on the pearls against the rodlike bones of her neck, snowballs of glamour trying to hide the winter trees of her age, and he wonders if he'll eat the pot roast because his wife made it or if he made her his wife because he likes pot roast. As he follows her toward the kitchen he feels himself topple into the idea, as moist as it is desiccated, that maybe what's missing is what his marriage had in the beginning, whatever that may have been.

Instead of the kitchen door it's the Plymouth door he slams behind him as he drives away from the house, the house on Pine Street that he's lived in for four years, since the days when his second son was still cute. He drives through Bell Port, mind flooded with the incongruous images of a big head, buck teeth, and a baseball, planning to drive farther, he doesn't know where, to wherever a man isn't missing whatever he's missing. Then he remembers that he doesn't know how to drive anywhere but Bell Port and turns back.

He parks at Fred Rutherford's and finds Fred entertaining two women, Mrs. Mondello and Miss Landers, one old and ridiculous, the other young and supple. Cocktails, ice, conversations Ward doesn't hear, until he hears himself telling them about his feeling that something's missing. He hears Fred, "You know what's missing from your life, Ward old man, is a boy to brag about, like my Clarence." The Mondello woman, "Oh no, Mr. Cleaver, what you're missing is a boy to fret over neurotically, like my Larry." Then the younger one leans close to him. Hot breath, the smell of chalk dust. He isn't sure what she says, but he's flooded by a feeling, as turgid as it is flaccid, that he's found what he's missing.

In her sunless room, Ward unsnaps her bra with a sound like a rubber band hitting the blackboard from the back of the classroom. Seeing her breasts he thinks grotesquely of a pot roast, Larry Mondello's girth, a baseball. He knows what's expected of him now, but he also knows that this is not what he's missing. He thinks about God and wonders if he's having a crisis of faith, but then realizes he doesn't know what faith he belongs to any more than he knows what state he lives in. In his sudden frustration he wants to force Miss Landers to perform a degrading sex act on him, but he doesn't know of any and leaves.

On the street, Ward is conscious that every eye is on him, not only the brown ones with flecks but the blue ones, even the hazel, and they all see that he left his wife, that he unsnapped the schoolteacher's bra, that he thought about Larry Mondello. He wants to think penetrating thoughts about how sterile and suffocating the upper-middle-class suburbs are, but he can't think of anything that hasn't already been said better by John Cheever. Then in the dimming street a rush of letterman sweaters, Brylcreem, boys playing basketball. Ward taking the ball, laying up, remembering when he played the game, and he realizes that whatever he's missing has something to do with young boys and balls. But then he's taking over the game, criticizing their hook shots, until one after another the boys hear their mothers calling and vanish into the murky dusk. Ward wonders what it means that he can't hear any mothers, not even his own.

A shrill voice from across the street, Whitey Whitney. "Hey, didja hear? Mrs. Cleaver got plastered and drownded the Beaver!" Ward doesn't know how he's supposed to react, he only knows he'll be expected to go home. But once there, he finds June sober, pot roast sliding out of the oven as warm and dark as the Langleys' Negro maid, Beaver banging through the screen door. She says the gossip's been garbled, she only got flustered and grounded the Beaver. Ward doesn't know if he's supposed to stay there now, but the smell of the pot roast hits him and he sits at the table.

Night, in the den, Ward sits at his desk, brown eyes gliding like eyes over the shelves, gliding to the empty space on the second shelf from the top. Then the feeling floods him, a feeling heavy and obscure with adjectives, that he knows what's been missing all along. The baseball.

The autographed baseball his Uncle Frank gave him when he was seventeen, white skin marked by Babe Ruth and Lou Gehrig, Lefty Grove and Ki Ki Cuyler. He realizes that Beaver must have taken it, that he should go ask him. But he doesn't know if getting it back will really kill the feeling of something missing or if he'll only learn that even the baseball can't make him whole. He sits, looking at the space on the shelf as it looks back at him, as empty as Miss Landers's bra.

Tag: Wally at the mirror, comb pumping like a dribbled basketball. Beaver behind on the bed, his whine like the wind around the eaves of a Cape Cod cottage. "Gee, Wally, do you think Dad will ever figure out that me and Larry were playing catch with his autographed baseball and it got runned over by a truck?" "I dunno, Beav," Wally says. "I guess we'll have to wait for the sequel." He turns out the light, and the gloaming luminescence that rises from nowhere like a mist of disquiet and memory obscures the fact that everything about the room is utterly mundane.

September 11-12, 1963

Everyone spent the rest of the afternoon deriding Updike's script for being impenetrably dull and pretentious, except for Hugh Beaumont, who had been strangely quiet and lost in thought since he had read it.

At last a messenger arrived from CBS. It was the word that everybody had most dreaded. Although the network's executives appreciated the fact that a prominent young journalist had declared *Beaver* "hip," they had decided to pass because they didn't know what "hip" meant.

Now there truly seemed to be no more hope. Once again, the tents on the Gomalco lot began to come down. Once again, sleeping bags were rolled and ground cloths were folded. But then Hugh Beaumont stirred from his deep thoughts and rose to his feet. Anyone else might have been ignored, but for Hugh they all stopped and listened. "As much as I've enjoyed all the literary submissions we've been receiving this summer," he announced, "none shook me like this one. After reading Mr. Updike's script, I finally realize what depth the figure of the suburban home owner contains, and how much can be said about modern society by exploring his inner life. I finally see what a meaningful statement I can make by portraying Ward. We cannot allow *Leave It to Beaver* to die. We have to exhaust every possibility before we surrender!"

For a long moment, no one stirred. Then they all turned back to their tents. But this time, the tents began to rise again.

All through the night and the next morning, countless ideas were floated as to how to bring Beaver back to life. But it was the arrival of a script in the next day's mail that gave them their first solid plan: not Gore Vidal's *The Best Beaver,* William Styron's *The Confessions of Beav Cleaver*, or Aldous Huxley's *Beavers of Perception*, but the final work of the venerable W. Somerset Maugham before he passed entirely through the door of senility.

The Beav and Sixpence

W. Somerset Maugham

Beaver arrives wearily at the concession stand at Friend's Lake after a long journey by steamer and prahu, sampan and rickshaw. On the verandah, overshadowed by coconut trees, flowering creepers, areca palms, and wild sago with its leaves like ostrich feathers, are a group of picnic tables. At one sit Whitey, Larry, and Gilbert, drinking stengahs and waiting for a fourth hand for bridge. At another, nearly lost in the shadow of a mango tree, sits a scrawny, bearded man, surrounded by a stack of mysterious objects.

Beaver orders a gin pahit and joins the others for bridge. He's come because his father is said to have vanished into the jungle beyond this lake, having conceived a sudden mad passion to abandon his family and become a painter. Beaver is not sure what he wants from his father if he finds him, but he has always felt strangely drawn to stories about the small grotesqueries of human nature. As if sensing this, his companions, as they bid and call, begin to tell him their own stories, the way boys will reveal things when far from home that they would never want heard by the local vicar or Miss Landers.

Whitey tells him of his obsessive, masochistic love for Judy Hensler, who wheedled money out of him and took pleasure in humiliating him, then prostituted herself and blamed him for not being man enough to keep her. At last he shot her dead. Beaver is skeptical, but Whitey pulls the gun from his pocket to prove it. Then, as if unable to resist some strange compulsion, he shoots himself in the head.

Now having only three players, they switch to poker. Gilbert narrates the story of his friendship with Richard, his private secretary and traveling companion. They were sublimely happy, for reasons that need not be discussed, until rumors began swirling about their "arrangement." Richard announced that he was going to ask Violet Rutherford to meet him at the soda fountain in order to maintain his respectability. Suddenly Gilbert found himself, not through jealousy so much as a strange compulsion to save the purely beautiful Richard from the degradations of conventionality, driving a kriss through his heart. Beaver is again skeptical, but Gilbert pulls the kriss out of his pocket and slashes his own throat from ear to ear.

Having only two players, Beaver and Larry switch to old maid. Larry leaps into the story of how, in order to maintain his respectability, he tried to conceal from his parents his native mistress and the half-caste infant she bore him. He made her crawl out through his bedroom window, but she, unable to bear the shame, strangled her child, set fire to his house, and hung herself from a rubber tree, where Larry found her the next morning, not only dead but vulcanized. Larry stands and says he has to get home. "Aren't you going to commit suicide?" Beaver asks.

"I'm thinking about it," Larry says, "but first I want to find out what my mom's making for dinner."

Beaver orders another gin prahit and plays solitaire. At last the scrawny, bearded man emerges from the mango's shadow, trying to sell him the paintings he's carrying with him. Beaver realizes that it's his father, reduced to a sallow, half-mad ghost of himself by his obsession with painting. He can't, however, bring himself to say anything, at least not until he looks at the paintings. Each one depicts a big-headed boy with a baseball cap and buck teeth. He asks who it is, but the man can only say that he is haunted by a weird memory of sitting in some sort of office and giving that boy a lecture on handling money responsibly. Most haunting of all is that he knows now that that was the last happy moment of his life.

Suddenly a flash of recognition fills his eyes. "Beaver?" he gasps. "Yes, Dad," Beaver says. "There's one thing you have to tell me," Ward says with desperate urgency, "one thing I have to know." "What's that, Dad?" "The twenty dollars Aunt Martha sent you for your birthday," Ward croaks, "did you put half of it in your savings account?" But before his son can ease his mind, the ruined man drops dead.

Beaver nurses his cocktail and thinks how tragic and pointless it is that so many men must lose their lives to cheap irony. Just then his attention is caught by a girl wearing only a lava-lava. He's about to wave her away, assuming she's just another of those half-caste women who haunt every concession stand at every tawdry little lake resort. Then he takes a closer look and realizes it's Violet Rutherford.

Violet agrees with him about irony. In fact, she tells him, it's terribly ironic that Gilbert should kill Richard over her, because she could never have been available to Richard anyway, not with her own strange and unspoken relationship with her brother Clarence. Whom, she reveals, she recently ran over in their father's station wagon, rendering him, for the first and last time in his life, truly lumpy. Then she sticks her head in Friend's Lake until she drowns.

Beaver sips his gin and gazes out into the relentless rain.

Tag: The boys turn out the light and look at each other from their respective beds. Suddenly realizing the unnatural desires that have bubbled all this time beneath their repressed exteriors, they smother each other to death with pillows.

September 12-15, 1963

Little alabaster Stanley Fafara exclaimed, "Why, of course! The British! The BBC is known for creating intelligent, artful TV shows that put American schlock to shame. Surely they'll leap at the chance to produce a British *Beaver* based on this script!" "Fab!" chirped Veronica Cartwright, who played Lumpy's little sister Violet. "And British things are becoming so gear that it would probably be re-shown over here!" Immediately, Hugh sent a cable to London.

Excited to realize that there was life beyond the three networks, everyone on the cast and crew gained a new élan. The tent city came back to life. Sue Randall revived the tradition of Tuesday-night entertainment with a spirited game of charades, in which all the answers were the titles of *Leave It to Beaver* episodes. Everybody agreed that Frank Bank's miming of the classic episode *In the Soup* was the standout performance.

As if to underscore the mood at Gomalco, over the next few days a number of ebullient pop songs arrived from some of the world's great performers. Among them were *The Beaver from Ipanema* by Antonio Carlos Jobim and

Stan Getz, *(You Ain't Nothin' But a) Beaver* by Elvis Presley, *Cast Your Beaver to the Winds* by Vince Guaraldi, and *A Taste of Beaver* by Herb Alpert and the Tijuana Brass.

Adding to the colorful festivities, a pair of Pop artists contributed their own Beaverabilia. Robert Rauschenberg sent a telegram saying, "This is a portrait of the Cleavers if I say so." Jasper Johns sent in a painting of an American flag that had fifty-one stars, presumably indicating that since Mayfield and Bell Port were apparently not situated in any of the fifty states, the actual number of states in the union must be fifty-one.

Literary submissions that arrived during those same days included Edna Ferber's *So Beaver*, John Rechy's *Suburb of Night*, Dr. Benjamin Spock's *Beaver and Wally Care*, Sloan Wilson's *The Boy in the Gray Flannel Baseball Cap,* and a protégé's tribute to that neurasthenic connoisseur of the horrific, H. P. Lovecraft.

The Mayfield Horror

by August Derleth in the manner of

H. P. Lovecraft

When a traveler takes the wrong turn at Camelback Cutoff just beyond Friend's Lake he comes upon a shunned and curious country. Outsiders seldom visit Mayfield of the monotonous clime and circumscribed lives, and since the horror of 1957 even the road signs pointing toward it have been taken down.

It is in Mayfield in a house not remarkable for its olfactory immaculateness that Larry Mondello is born to Mrs. Mondello, of the decayed Mondellos. Of the father nothing is known, nor is any doctor or midwife known to have attended upon this birth. Those who catch a glimpse of the infant come away revolted by his distinctly porcine appearance. By the age of two the boy is as pudgy as a child of ten, and by the age of ten he is eating his mother out of house and home and working his way through the blasphemous books that he's inherited through two centuries of Mondellos, volumes that reek of amorphous horrors and hint of the Different Ones.

When Larry is thirteen years of age he appears one evening at the Cleaver household in quest of a dreaded volume kept under lock and key in Ward's den—the hideous *Castornomicon*. Ward, of the undecayed Cleavers, can't help looking at the foetid lad with abhorrence. "Whatever for do you need to look at the *Castornomicon*, Larry?"

"Gee, Mr. Cleaver," Larry says, speaking in a strange, porcine fashion that sounds only partly of mankind. "I just need to read about a certain incantation and junk." Ward looks at the accursed lad and a wave of loathing takes him. "This incantation wouldn't be the Dho formula, would it?" Larry shakes his head fervently. "Gosh, no, Mr. Cleaver. What would I want with…whatever that is?" Ward, now fairly shaking with revulsion, gibbers, "I'm afraid I can't let you see it, Larry. It's just not suitable for boys your age." Larry, looking despondent in a porcine way, reluctantly takes his leave.

In the small hours that very night, the Cleavers are awakened by the wild cries of the savage watchdog that patrols the house next door. Then there rings out a scream so loathsome that it raises half the sleepers of Mayfield and haunts their dreams ever afterward.

The family, belting on their robes, hastens outside. And there, under the jimmied window to Ward's den, they come upon the watchdog, crouching over all that remains of Larry Mondello: a foetid mound of frogs, snails, and apple cores.

Yet all this is only the prologue to the actual Mayfield horror. It is on the very next night that the nameless thing bursts loose. About six o'clock, Whitey Whitney, of the half-decayed Whitneys, rushes frenziedly back from the store where he had gone to buy a carton of milk for his mother. He is convulsed with fright as he gibbers, "I walked by Larry's house and it came shambling out, mom! It had a goatish growth on its chin like some kind of ichor, and it was making this daemoniac sound with its tentacles!"

Word quickly spreads through Mayfield, and noon of the next day finds the still-undecayed Cleavers and the newly decayed Rutherfords trooping over the roads listening for the nameless snapping sound Whitey had described, and crinkling their noses at the foeter of sandaled feet. "What do you think, Ward old man?" Fred Rutherford gibbers. "Does a Different One walk amongst us?" Ward can only nod. Beaver, Wally, and the manifestly decayed Lumpy gaze at each other in ever-mounting waves of horror.

Ward, however, has a plan for dealing with the nameless, non-Euclidian threat. Unknown to any of his companions, the night before he had sifted through the unmentionable remains of Larry Mondello and found the lad's diary under the frogs and snails. The notations therein were in the hideous form of a rebus and written— not, as he would have expected, in a language of great antiquity— but in plain English. But with the aid of the dread *Castornomicon* he'd managed to decode its eldritch meaning.

"This is neat," the diary reads. "Yog-Sothoth says all I gotta do is say the Dho formula and summon the rest of the Different Ones. They'll clear off the Wholesome Ones, and then I can eat anything I want!"

Forewarned, Ward has memorized an incantation from the monstrous *Castornomicon*, and when shortly they come upon the goateed form of Yog-Sothoth in front of a coffee house he is ready. In a voice choking with horror, he ululates the foul syllables: "*Ygniih. Ygnaiih. Thflthka'ngha.* Away misfit! Away!"

With a cataclysmic peal and the foeter of burning hair, Yog-Sothoth returns to the nameless blankness of primal time.

Tag: The boys pull their blankets up to their chins. Beaver says, "Gee, Wally. What kind of name is Yog-Sothoth, anyway?" "I dunno, Beav," Wally says. "I think it's one of those beatnik names. Like Maynard." The mere evocation of the names fills the boys with ever-mounting paroxysms of such a cosmically daemonic, soul-devouring horror that they pass the entire night with the light on.

September 15-16, 1963

Most of the cast simply dismissed it as non-Euclidian nonsense, but it left Rusty Stevens thoughtful. "Gee," he whined, "it sure is crummy how these big-name writers keep killing off characters. Don't they get what a *series* is all about?" "Oh well," cracked Stephen Talbot, whose character Gilbert Bates had eclipsed Larry Mondello as Beaver's best friend in the last two seasons, "at least it's nobody important this time!" Rusty tried to punch him in the stomach, but Stephen only jumped away, laughing obnoxiously.

As these innocent hijinks occupied the cast's attention, producers Bob Mosher and Joe Connelly were percolating thoughts of their own. Mosher remembered, "Me and Joe, we knew it had just the angle that *Beaver* needed. By Jiminy, if we could just mix the Cleavers with monsters, we knew we'd have something!" Knowing that many independent TV stations were having great success with old monster movies, they imagined a bright future for the show in syndication.

Their timing was perfect, because just then a cable arrived from London. The BBC said that they had briefly considered resurrecting the show as an educational children's program by turning Beaver into a mysterious figure who leads his companions on adventures through space and time. But upon realizing that Beaver Cleaver would be an utterly unbelievable character if he ventured outside the American suburbs or to any date prior to 1950, they chose to retool the idea with a hero of their own devising. Mosher and Connelly immediately got on the phone and began calling friends in the field of syndicated programming.

The next day's mail brought what would turn out to be the last contribution by a musician to the *Beaver* cause, although no one then realized it. During the summer, some of America's greatest songwriters had submitted new sets of lyrics to be sung to the *Leave It to Beaver* theme song originally composed by Dave Kahn. Their ranks were now joined by rambling, radical folk singer Woody Guthrie.

> *This Mayfield is your Mayfield,*
> *This is your Bell Port too.*
> *From Crystal Falls to Camelback*
> *There's nowhere else for you.*
> *Ain't no redwoods,*
> *Junk like that's all gone.*
> *No waving wheat,*
> *Just a hunk of lawn.*
> *I went walking along Grant Ave,*
> *Past school and bridge and Gus.*
> *I saw so little to sing about*
> *Next time I'll take the bus.*

Although troubled by its implicit critique of private property, everyone agreed that it was a fine tune to sing along to, and Sue Randall promised to make it the centerpiece of her next Tuesday-night hoedown.

Although troubled by its implicit critique of private property, everyone agreed that it was a fine tune to sing along to, and Sue Randall promised to make it the centerpiece of her next Tuesday-night hoedown.

Scripts and books arriving that day included Helen Gurley Brown's *Sex and the Single Beaver*, William Lederer and Eugene Burdick's *The Ugly Beaver*, and Dr. Alfred Kinsey's *Sexual Behavior in the Human Beaver*. Also among them was an homage to Thomas Mann written by the great novelist's son. Angelus Mann had long felt a deep affinity for the youngest Cleaver child, for just as Beaver had earned his nickname by being unable to pronounce "Theodore" as a little boy, so had the young Mann, struggling to pronounce his own name, earned the lifelong nickname "Golo."

Death in Mayfield

by Golo Mann in the manner of
Thomas Mann

Having just been promoted at work, Ward knows that he stands at the pinnacle of his career, and that men who have long called him Ward will now be calling him Mr. Cleaver. "You're a master of diligent control and restraint," says his boss, Mr. Anderson. "Why, you're a regular Apollo, that's what you are!" Ward thanks him and wishes he had studied more Greek mythology.

For all that, Ward is troubled. Lately he has found it increasingly difficult to study his portfolios, and it unsettles him that the piles on his desk are approaching disorder. He takes a long, solitary walk to settle his mind, but as he passes the Mayfield Cemetery he sees Gus the Fireman standing in ghastly silence, beckoning him with a single finger. Ward decides that it is time for a vacation.

He arrives at Friend's Lake to find it crowded with gaily dressed holidaymakers. Among them he is appalled to see Fred Rutherford, attempting to ingratiate himself with his son Lumpy and his teenage friends by dressing pitifully and absurdly in blue jeans, t-shirt, and sneakers. Ward congratulates himself for having the judgment to dress as a man of his age and station should dress on vacation, in suit, tie, and gleaming black oxfords.

As he settles down to read the newspaper, his eye is drawn to the family gathering for a picnic at the edge of the lake. He recognizes the simpering Mrs. Mondello and her drearily affected teenage daughter. Joining them last, his arms full of corn dogs, is the young prince of the family.

Ward has seen Larry Mondello countless times before and felt nothing for him but a vague distaste, but until now he has never seen him wearing only swimming trunks. Awash in the vast, pale sweep of Larry's flesh, the abandoned voluptuousness of his sheer corpulence, Ward is surprised to find himself strangely transfixed. He tells himself that he must surely be appreciating Larry at an aesthetic level. He wonders if Larry is the Platonic ideal of something and wishes he had studied more classical philosophy along with the Greek mythology.

When Larry waddles back toward the concessions stand for more corn dogs, Ward finds himself compelled to hurry ahead in order to intercept him there. He is puzzled and disturbed to find the stand manned by Gus the Fireman. "What are you doing here, Gus?" he demands. "I'm likely to show up when you least expect," Gus says. "Like Goethe's Mephistopheles. Have a corn dog."

Ward wishes he had studied more eighteenth century German literature along with the classical philosophy and the Greek mythology. He also wishes he had studied more Nietzsche, Wagner, Biblical symbolism, early Enlightenment cultural history, and esoteric alchemical texts, just in case. He purchases a bag of potato chips and hurries away, suddenly dreading the very encounter with Larry that he had sought. Watching the boy's flesh roll as he waddles back to his family, arms filled once again with corn dogs, Ward finds himself overcome by dizziness. He blames the heat and decides he should drive home, but as he comes to his car he realizes that he has left his briefcase on the lawn by the lake. He rushes back with a fervent exhilaration.

On the way, he overhears two teenage lifeguards whispering conspiratorially: the corn dogs have gone bad, but Gus insists that the fact be kept secret in order to avoid a panic. Ward immediately knows that he should warn Mrs. Mondello, but he also realizes that if he does so she will flee immediately, taking her son with her. When he reaches the lake again and sees Larry pushing a corn dog into his mouth with a religious concentration, Ward cannot bring himself to speak.

Larry catches Ward gazing at him, and immediately he heaves himself to his feet and begins waddling back toward the concession stand. With heart in throat, Ward wonders if the boy wants him to follow. It strikes him that if he is to meet Larry alone, he should look younger and more attractive—and so he steals the blue jeans, t-shirt, and sneakers that he finds abandoned by Fred Rutherford and, unaware of how absurd and pitiful he has become, hurries after the object of his devotion. But Larry has vanished. Ward searches for him with a frantic urgency until he collapses to the shore of the lake.

Tag: Wally, Beaver, and Ward are engaging in a pillow fight in the boys' room. Ward fights with an almost violent eagerness, but Wally and Beaver look increasingly uncomfortable. At last Beaver says, "Gee, Dad, it's neat that you feel better after the corn dog and junk…but aren't you kinda old for this?" Ward doffs his baseball cap and letterman sweater, gives Wally back his Bob Cousy P. F. Flyers, and shuffles mournfully out of the room.

September 16-20, 1963

"This adaptation of a great European novel gives me an excellent idea," said Doris Packer, who played Mrs. Rayburn, the principal of Grant Avenue Grammar School. "We should use this to interest National Educational Television. Of course, it won't pay nearly as well as a commercial network, but think of how it will improve the lives of children across America!" As one, all the juvenile actors on the show curled their lips. But Richard Deacon, who played Lumpy's pompous father Fred Rutherford, was so taken with the idea that he took it upon himself to petition the NET offices.

This was especially good timing, as Mosher and Connelly were quickly learning that the syndication market was closed to them— ironically because local stations had already committed to reruns of the first six seasons of *Leave It to Beaver*. "We have no doubt that the new season you're proposing would be the most exciting and original of all," an executive at Group W Broadcasting explained, "but we just can't miss the opportunity to bring the young, cute Jerry Mathers back to the American viewing public, complete with normal-sized head."

Although submissions continued to arrive in the mail, it soon became evident that since Woody Guthrie's lyrics nothing had come from any musician, painter, toymaker, or anyone else other than a writer. It was Barbara Billingsley who first realized why: as the news of *Beaver*'s cancellation had spread, artists, film makers, and just about everybody else had realized that there was no point in contributing anything new. Writers, with their heads habitually stuck in the sand, were always the last ones to catch on to anything.

"Luckily for us," added Hugh Beaumont with a slightly forced enthusiasm, "or we wouldn't keep getting these exciting scripts to keep our spirits up!"

Among those exciting scripts were Fletcher Knebel and Charles W. Bailey's *Seven Days in Mayfield,* Thornton Wilder's *The Bridge of Avenue Grant,* Kyle Onstott's *Beaverdingo,* and Edith Lewis's loving tribute to Willa Cather, *Death Comes to the Archbeaver.* But the most significant of them would turn out to be that from the bedridden mistress of Southern Grotesque, Flannery O'Connor.

A Good Beaver Is Hard to Find

Flannery O'Connor

Uncle Billy and the Cleaver family climb into Ward's car for a drive up to Friend's Lake. Uncle Billy, squeezed in between the boys in the back seat, says, "Maybe we oughtn't to go to Friend's Lake. They say that escaped felon, the one they call the Creep, was seen up there. Not that I'm afraid, mind you. When I was a sheriff in Georgia that time I tangled with plenty of creeps."

Ward and June exchange a glance. Although June's face is as broad and innocuous as a cabbage, it's plain that she's thinking, "God, I hope the boys don't believe everything this old windbag says."

"Gee, Uncle Billy," Beaver says, "I didn't know you were a sheriff." "Sure was," Uncle Billy says. "Did I tell you boys about that time I roped in a crazy fellow that had blinded himself with lye?"

Ward, wearing a yellow golf sweater with bright blue parrots designed into it, harrumphs loudly. "Maybe we ought to change the subject, Uncle Billy." "Gee, dad," Wally says, "not when the story's just getting good!" Uncle Billy chuckles and says, "Oh, I've got plenty of good ones. One time I had to arrest an old man for bashing his little granddaughter's head against a rock until she was deader than a mackerel."

Ward swerves off the road with a screech of tires and pulls up to a diner. They all go in and order Co'-Colas. The waitress tells them that another person has spotted the Creep in the vicinity of Friend's Lake. "That's where we're going!" Beaver pipes in. "Ain't you folks scairt?" the waitress asks. "Heck, no," Wally says. "Not when we've got Uncle Billy with us!"

As they climb back into the car, June whispers, "Ward, I'm worried that your uncle's stories may be a bad influence on the boys." "Oh, now, June," he says, "I'm sure he's run out of tall tales by now." But as soon as they drive off, Uncle Bill says, "Did I tell you boys about the time a bull gored a lady right in the heart? Killed her deader than a mackerel. It happened near here. Folks used to say that bull was really Christ."

"Uncle Billy, please!" Ward hollers, but Wally quickly puts in, "Aw, gee, dad. Don't go ape on Uncle Billy. I want to hear more about the bull that's really Christ." "Me, too!" Beaver shrills loudly.

"Take that left coming up," Uncle Billy says. "That'll take us to where that lady got gored. I believe that old bull that's really Christ still roams those woods." Ward is about to pass the turn-off, but the trio in the back seat set up such a clamor that he reluctantly gives in. As they drive into the woods one of the tires blows out. They all pile out and Ward, grumbling, gets the jack out of the trunk. "I sure wish the bull that's really Christ would show up now," Wally says.

Instead of the bull, however, three men suddenly emerge from the trees, all holding guns. Their leader, with a head of wavy blond hair, is obviously the Creep. "Sorry, Gertrude," he says, "but we'll be taking that jalopy now."

"I don't get it," Beaver says to the Creep. "I thought you were supposed to be up at Friend's Lake." "You really *don't* get it, do you, Beav?" Wally asks. "This is one of those ironic twists that I learned about in creative writing class."

The Creep tells one of his cronies to take Ward and Wally into the woods. They trudge off, and a moment later a shot is heard. Then another.

"Oh, gosh, Mister Creep," whines Uncle Billy. "Please don't kill me." Beaver looks disdainfully at him, understanding at last that his hero is really just a blowhard. Then the Creep orders his other crony to take June and Beaver into the woods. As soon as they disappear from sight, two closely spaced shots are heard.

The Creep then lifts his gun and points it directly at Uncle Billy's head. A shot rings out, but it's the Creep who's been hit, taking a bullet to his gun hand. The four Cleavers come walking out of the woods.

"What's the big idea, Claude?" yells the Creep, clutching his hand. "You're supposed to be dead!" "Nah," Wally says. "Me and dad disarmed the first guy and fired two shots into the air so you'd think we'd been finished off." Beaver picks up the story. "And then Dad took the other guy's gun and fired two more shots into the air when me and Mom showed up!"

While the boys round up their prisoners, Ward good-naturedly resumes work on the flat tire.

Tag: The boys are getting ready for bed. "Gee, Wally," Beaver says. "Do you suppose there honest-to-goodness is a bull who's really Christ?" "I don't know, Beav," Wally says. "Uncle Billy can be a real windbag sometimes." Wally flicks off the light switch, but the fluorescent red paint on the life-size crucifix makes the room glow luridly.

September 20-21, 1963

Then, after days of cautious optimism, two terrible blows struck at once. First, NET refused their advances. Although impressed by the educational value of the Mann script, they had already committed to a new season of *The French Chef* and didn't feel they could take on both projects. That same day, the executives of Gomalco Studios announced that they had run out of patience with the "okie camp" occupying their lot. The *Beaver* loyalists were ordered to evacuate immediately.

For most of the residents of the camp this was the final blow. When Hugh Beaumont announced that he had seen this coming and was already finalizing arrangements to lease a new headquarters for their cause, a few voices cheered. But the great majority of his comrades had had enough. Those who decided it was time to go home and get on with their lives included the entire crew, along with writers Dick Conway and Roland MacLane, musicologist Pete Rugolo, make-up whiz Jack Barron, director Norman Tokar, and cast members Veronica (Violet Rutherford) Cartwright, Madge (Mrs. Mondello) Blake, Doris (Mrs. Rayburn) Packer, Burt (Gus the Fireman) Mustin, Richard (Richard Rickover) Correll, and Stephen (Gilbert Bates)

Talbot. Mosher and Connelly were devastated. Connelly recalled, "Me and Bob, we didn't know how we could possibly keep going without Burt Mustin. Jeepers, we hadn't felt so shaken since Tiger Fafara left, taking the character of Tooey Brown from us forever."

Those who would remain loyal to Hugh's dream stood back and watched their former colleagues disappear into the smoggy Hollywood afternoon. Lovely Sue Randall began to weep quietly. "Oh Hugh," she sniffed, "it was wonderful of you to find a new place from which to continue our fight. But what are we going to do? Everyone's turned us down."

Tony Dow pounded a fist into his palm and said, "I wouldn't be so sure about that! That script by that Southern lady, Miss O'Connor, got me thinking. If *Beaver* can appeal to Southerners, why can't it appeal to other races too? Aren't there UHF stations right here in town for Mexicans and Negroes?" A grin split Hugh's face and he slapped his surrogate son on the shoulder. "That's thinking, my boy!"

That very night they moved into their new headquarters, a four-bedroom (plus den) house on a quiet suburban street in the San Fernando Valley. Barbara Billingsley remarked that perhaps the mass defection of their former allies hadn't been such a bad thing after all, as the house would have been awfully crowded with everyone in it.

Hugh made sure to leave their forwarding address with the receptionist at Gomalco so they wouldn't miss out on any new submissions from the literary community. Just as he was leaving, the mailman delivered the last script to be opened on that historic lot: the work of recovering alcoholic and lesbian enthusiast John O'Hara.

Appointment in Bell Port

John O'Hara

DEATH SPEAKS:

There was a teenager in Mayfield who sent his little brother to the store to buy him a soft drink and in a little while the little brother came back, white and trembling, and said, "Wally, just now at the store Death gave me a creepy look! Lend me your bike so I can ride to Bell Port where Death won't find me!" The teenager lent him his bike, and the little brother pedaled away. Then the teenager went to the store and saw me standing there and said, "Why did you give my little brother a creepy look?" That was not a creepy look, I said, it was only a start of surprise. I was astonished to see him in Mayfield, for I have an appointment with him later today in Bell Port.

Word spreads like wildfire through Mayfield that Beaver Cleaver has thrown a glass of milk in Whitey Whitney's face.

"Jeezozz H. Kee-rist, Beav!" Wally says nasally. "What in heck did you do that for?" Beaver, who's recently been thrown out of prep school, mumbles, "Because he said my future wife, whoever she is, is going to cheat on me someday." "Well, heck yeah," Wally says, brushing his raccoon coat. "Spouses always cheat on each other." Beaver, looking distressed, takes a long pull from his flask. "But what if she turns out to be a lesbian?" he asks. And Wally responds, "Then she'll cheat on you with another lesbian."

Beaver, sodden with drink, walks the streets of Mayfield that night. As nearly as anybody can make out, Mayfield was founded by Swedes in 1748, who were subsequently massacred by an Indian tribe, and their original name for the settlement had been lost. Some believe it had been called Meatballfield, but others, particularly the Lantenengo Street crowd, pooh-pooh the notion. Beaver doesn't really give a damn. He just wants to get into Yale and marry a rich heterosexual woman who won't cheat on him.

At school the next morning, a hung-over Beaver asks Judy Hensler (of the coal Henslers, with an address on Lantenengo Street) to go out in the playground with him. All the other students see them leave together, even Judy's bootlegger boyfriend. It's tacitly assumed that they've snuck off to have a sexual encounter, even though it's generally believed that Judy is a lesbian. Beaver knows he's really gonna get it now.

A day later Beaver is talking about how desperately he wants to be accepted to Yale, when Larry Mondello interrupts him. Larry comes from one of the oldest families in Mayfield, dating back to the Revolutionary War. He tells Beaver that he's always hated him because he knows that Beaver will one day have an affair with his wife-to-be, whoever she is. Beaver hears him out, then punches him in the stomach. Several students look on with disapproval.

Believing that the entire town has turned against him for his erratic behavior, and concerned that the New Deal will ruin his family fortune, Beaver realizes that what he's really wanted all this time—especially since he'll probably never be accepted at Yale— was to kill himself. He thinks of climbing into the giant soup bowl and then jumping out, but he remembers how much trouble he got into the last time he climbed into it and drops the idea. Then he considers drowning himself in Miller's Pond, until he remembers that lesbians like to hang out there, and he'd feel embarrassed to have a bunch of icky dykes, even if many of them have Lantenengo Street addresses, looking at his corpse.

Finally he decides to asphyxiate himself. He climbs into his dad's Stutz Bearcat and turns on the starter. Luckily for him, the Stutz Bearcat is parked in the driveway, not in the garage. June, in an evening gown and short cape, finds him a few minutes later. "Why, Beaver," she says. "Why on earth are you sitting in your father's Stutz Bearcat with the motor running?" Beaver explains that he's trying to commit suicide. With a cry of dismay, June pulls him out of the Stutz Bearcat and drags him into his father's den.

Ward, glaring at Beaver across his desk in the den, sips from his flask and fiddles with his Phi Beta Kappa key. The son of a farmer from Shaker Heights, he put himself through prep school and earned a PhD in Philosophy at State College. He delivers a stern lecture on how inconsiderate suicide is to the other members of the family. Beaver promises to stop his boorish behavior and vows that he'll never try to kill himself again, not even if he never gets into Yale and the woman he will someday marry turns out to be an adulterous lesbian.

Tag: Wally, Beaver, and Death are preparing for bed. "Hey, Death," Beaver says. "Why did you tell my brother you had an appointment with me in Bell Port?" "Sorry, Beav," Death says. "It was Lumpy Rutherford—of the railroad Rutherfords—I had an appointment with, not you. I must have been thinking about something else." "Like what?" Wally asks. "Oh, I don't know," Death muses. "Maybe I was wondering if the Langleys' Negro maid is a lesbian." They all laugh and get into a three-way pillow fight.

September 21-22, 1963

Upon moving into their new house, the gang celebrated with an impromptu performance of the O'Hara script. Rusty Stevens and Jerry Mathers teased Jeri Weil, who played Beaver's classmate Judy Hensler, about being a lesbian, but since none of them knew what the word meant, no harm was done.

Apart from those three, only ten people were left in the loyal band: Hugh Beaumont, Barbara Billingsley, and Tony Dow, who comprised the rest of the Cleaver family; Ken Osmond, Frank Bank, and little milky Stanley Fafara, who played the friends of the boys; and Richard Deacon, Sue Randall, and series creators Bob Mosher and Joe Connelly themselves.

While Sue and Jeri were dispatched to buy groceries, Barbara led the rest of the group in decorating their new abode. When they'd left Gomalco, Hugh had appropriated many of the submissions that had arrived during the summer, so the walls were soon gaily festooned with such mementos of their odyssey as Salvador Dali's wax mustache, Beaver-themed paintings by Miró, Warhol, Nieman, and Rockwell, and Jasper Johns's fifty-one starred flag. The rooms were all decked out with Claes Oldenburg's furniture in the form of various foodstuffs.

The younger boys were assigned one of the bedrooms, the teens another, the men a third, and the women and Jeri Weil the last. Before retiring that night, all the youngsters phoned their parents to get permission to live there indefinitely. The adults notified their spouses that they'd be away for a spell, but promised that they'd be home in triumph just as soon as they'd succeeded in finding a new home for *Leave It to Beaver*.

The next day, a package of submissions was forwarded from Gomalco. The first scripts and books opened at their new digs included John Le Carré's *The Creep Who Came in from the Cold*, Bishop James Pike's *If Beaver Be Heresy*, Albert Schweitzer's homage to Goethe, *The Sorrows of Young Wallace*, and the gang's favorite: sensualist, gourmand, and mountaineer James Salter's *A Beaver and a Pastime*. Serendipitously, Salter's evocation of the search for the real America resonated with their own warm feelings about having left the glitz of Hollywood for the suburban bliss of the San Fernando Valley.

A Beaver and a Pastime

James Salter

(Eddie narrates.)

Bell Port. The blue, somnolent town. Its station wagons. Its soda fountains. I pass the *quai,* walk along the Rue de Main. When I come to the Methodist church I turn onto a street canopied with trees. I pass a young girl. She has a thin face, a passionate face, the face of a girl who might move to Mayfield.

The Rutherfords' summer house is just ahead. The season has ended, and they have gone back to their elegant lives, leaving the house to my use. The garden has withered. There's a Pissarro-like silence. I am eighteen. The years are dry as Wonder Bread.

Suddenly Wally is there. He's driven up in Lumpy's jalopy. He has a pug nose and wide-set, not particularly intelligent eyes. It's of schoolboy heroes that he reminds me, boys from the east, quarterbacks, coxswains, slender as girls. He has come, he says, to see the real America.

We go on a walking tour of Bell Port. The diners, where the sandwiches come wrapped in wax paper. The Place de Maple. The Champs de Elm. The little shops, their windows resplendent with Schwinn bikes, cha-cha records in their lurid sleeves, mannequins decked out in poodle skirts. We pass a field where graceful boys fling a football around. A cemetery. Discarded baseball cards skitter across a weed-grown lot. Wally takes it all in avidly.

It is in the malt shop that he first sees her. In her cheerleader outfit and saddle shoes, she is catastrophically lovely. She is surrounded by boys in lettermen sweaters, all vying to buy her a malted. But when her eyes meet Wally's in the mirror, they all capitulate, like conscripts who know the battle is hopeless.

"I'll meet you back at the house, Eddie," he says, and I know I've lost him.

Of what comes next, some things I saw, some I discovered, and some I dreamed. I can no longer tell them apart. But the dreams, I know, are as true as Mrs. Cleaver's spotless kitchen. More true, perhaps. I am not telling the truth about Wally, I am making him up. I am creating him out of my own insecurities.

Early afternoon. She sits on the grass, leaning back on her arms, in the shadow of a bandstand. Wally is leaning across her body, and they are making out like track and field stars. He pauses at last. Her cheeks are flushed, her beehive in disarray. Wally kisses her ear, and then, as one stirs a favorite mare, he kisses her full on the lips again. It is these atrocities that induce them toward puppy love.

Wally parks the jalopy in the lee of a warehouse, overlooking the *quai*. The air smells of frying hamburger, the light through the windshield is sharp as cleats. She has let him slip his tongue into her mouth. Wally wonders if this counts as second base. Her breath smells of Juicy Fruit. With his tongue, Wally is abusing her like a sailor.

He thinks of taking her home, but is afraid his parents will disapprove of her. He can see his mother's troubled eyes. "But, Wally. She's from the provinces. Didn't you notice the scuff marks on her saddle shoes?" And there's another reason for putting off the trip. His father, he knows, will pressure him about starting his studies at State. Or Valley. State or Valley. He's had his fill of it.

They have dinner on the Avenue de Hill, in a diner filled with the clatter of plates, the thump-thump-thump of a jukebox. They stuff themselves with Sloppy Joes, onion rings, apple pie a la mode, specialties of a region known for its food. In the summer house, in Lumpy's room, she lets him cup her breast. He knows for a certainty he's reached second base. He shudders like a bull.

They go for a drive in the country, not turning back until they reach Camelback Cutoff. The sky is achingly blue, the clouds like pom-poms. She wants to talk of all the ways there are to pet.

Wally begins casually to list them, skirting the one he really desires. Finally he blurts it out.

"That would be getting to third base, *non*?" she asks.

"That would be getting to third base, *oui*," he says.

She grows pensive, and he fears he has offended her. But then, in the voice of a little girl, she says, "We must try it some time."

He expels his breath like a bull.

Driving to her house, Wally is killed in a motor accident. There are few details. Splinters of glass. The rain spattering down. Fuzzy dice balanced on his shattered chest. I cannot believe the news, even if I've been expecting it in the back of my mind. After all, I am dreaming the whole thing.

The one thing I know for sure is that I couldn't bear the thought of him sliding into home plate.

Tag: The boys' bedroom. Discarded clothes strewn about. An uncapped toothpaste tube. Beaver gets into bed. "Did you have a neat time in Bell Port?" he asks. Wally stares into space, doesn't answer. After a while Beaver flicks off the light. In the near-darkness, he hears Wally sigh like a bull. Or is he only dreaming Wally's presence?

September 22-23, 1963

After having fully settled into their new headquarters, the intrepid thirteen sat down to discuss their next move. Many of them had exciting suggestions and insights to add to Tony Dow's idea that they should adapt the show for UHF stations aimed at non-white audiences. Unfortunately, they soon had to abandon the idea as they realized that none of them had any idea how to approach Mexicans or Negroes. Barbara reminded them that they did know a person of color, having worked with Kim Hamilton, who played the Langleys' Negro maid in one episode in the sixth season, but as no one had kept her phone number, they had no idea how to contact her.

Breathing a sigh of relief, Rusty Stevens said that he'd always gotten Ds in Spanish and so doubted his ability to become fluent enough to perform on a Spanish station. "I mean, how the heck do you say, 'Gee, Beav,' in Spanish, anyway?" Ken Osmond was also glad to be off the hook, as he'd been concerned that he wouldn't look right in blackface.

"But gosh," Jerry Mathers said. "What other TV stations are left?" A silence fell over the group. After a few troubled moments, Richard Deacon slapped the table and said it was high time that they followed up on all the many offers they'd received over the summer from toy companies, cartoon producers, comic book publishers, and others eager to profit from the Cleaver franchise. "Why, if we can get a successful line of toys or a cartoon series out there," he said, "we'll have the networks lining up to put us back on the air!"

The others responded with unease. Bob Mosher said, "Me and Joe, we hated to go around with our hats in our hands. Jumping Jehoshaphat, just six months before we'd been sitting on top of the world." Ken Osmond feared that any possible markets would be wary of them if they seemed too desperate. Hugh Beaumont didn't want to seem greedy. Richard Deacon berated them for their lack of get-up-and-go, but the others could not be roused to enthusiasm.

The next day's mail brought more submissions, including *B.* by Thomas Pynchon, Marshall McLuhan's *The Beaver Is the Message,* and Frank Gruber's tribute to Zane Grey, *Riders of the Purple Beaver.* But the script that had the greatest impact came from hawkish, chain-smoking ideologue Ayn Rand.

Cleaver Shrugged

Ayn Rand

"Who is Ward Cleaver?" Those are the words everyone in Mayfield is asking. The town's economy is failing, law and order are collapsing, and rumors are spreading that it all started when the man named Ward Cleaver disappeared. Intellectuals realize that it was a chain reaction, that when Cleaver left his work in the inferior hands of Fred Rutherford their company began spiraling downward; and when Cleaver was no longer there to set an example for the other fathers in town, the animal mentality of Rutherford's son Lumpy spread through the populace. But where is this Cleaver, everyone asks, and why did he vanish?

Beaver takes it upon himself to find his father. He questions Lumpy, who responds with a long speech about how men like Ward Cleaver only think they're better than everyone else and nobody really needs them at all. But in the process he reveals how driven he is by the small man's envy, the hatred of the good for being the good.

Then Beaver runs to Miss Landers for comfort. She makes a long speech about how, now that things are going wrong, they need a powerful government to take care of them, which will impose higher taxes and stiffer regulations in order to protect the weak and destitute. But in the process she exposes the irrational disregard for individual free will that lies at the heart of all collectivism.

Beaver rushes away and is accosted by Eddie Haskell. He cackles and makes a long speech about how, with Ward Cleaver gone, he'll be free to give Beaver the business whenever he feels like it. But in the process he reveals how his concept of giving the business is founded on moral cowardice and a fear of the rationality which is the foundation of man's existence.

The distraught Beaver runs off into the hills above Friend's Lake. There, in a hidden valley beyond Crystal Falls, he discovers a community made up of remarkable men: the great physician Alex Stone, the great aeronautical engineer Steve Douglas, the great insurance salesman Jim Anderson, and the head of America's favorite family, Oswald Nelson. Each of them is famous not only as an expert in his field but as a father and a moral guide. The newest arrival is Ward Cleaver, whom Beaver finds sipping coffee and listening to the others explain their mission.

These great men have gone on strike in protest of a world of mediocrity, subjectivism, and taxation. "I won't have my three sons growing up in a world ruined by government interference," Steve Douglas growls. Now that mankind has begun to feel the loss of their intellectual superiority, they say, it's time to broadcast a long speech over the radio that will shake the world out of its apathy. Originally, they had intended for Jim Anderson to deliver it, but now he insists that no one is as expert at the calm but convincing lecture as Ward Cleaver. "And Jim knows best," adds Oswald Nelson with a crinkly grin.

As Beaver watches in anxious suspense, Ward sets down his coffee cup, takes the microphone and begins to speak to the world. But instead of the objectivist manifesto the other men expect, he delivers a brief, reasonable lecture about how the most important things in life are teamwork, a bit of humble self-sacrifice, responsibility, and consideration for others. "Individual rights are important," he concludes, "but we all have to follow rules we don't like sometimes, and we all have to pay our fair share, even when we think we're smarter than the other fellow."

The others are speechless. It's clear to them that their crusade is doomed. Beaver asks, "But gee, Dad. How come all the other dads are saying all that goofy junk about virtuous selfishness, absolute individualism, pure rationality, and uncontrolled capitalism?" Ward smiles gently and says, "Beaver, do you remember when you tried sleeping in a room of your own but you saw a shadow that you thought was a lion and ran back to Wally's room? Well, it's the same with grownups. When things change, people get scared, and they're liable to grab hold of the silliest ideas. Our job is just to sit them down and talk sensibly to them." Then he claps his hands and rubs them together eagerly, adding, "What do you say, big fella? Should we go home and get started?"

Tag: Beaver is troubled. "You know something, Wally? All these grown-up ideas about compromise and complexity and flexibility and junk make me nervous. I like things real simple, with one rule for everything so I know I'll always be right." "Gee, Beav," Wally says, "you can sure be a goofy little kid sometimes." Beaver turns off the light and smiles as all the subtle shades of gray in the room are reduced to a comforting black and white.

September 23-30, 1963

The cast was caught off guard by the script's denouement, considering its author. "Goodness," said Barbara Billingsley, "who'd have ever thought a right-wing polemicist like Ayn Rand would give Ward dialogue that really sounds like something he'd say, instead of just using him as a mouthpiece for her own ridiculous ideas?"

"Well," said Hugh Beaumont, setting his coffee cup down with a smile, "that's how you can tell a true artist, never letting her own politics lead her into being untrue to the reality of her characters."

"But gee," said Frank Bank, "there is something to what this Rand has to say. Aren't we just wallowing in our victimhood?" "Sure!" Ken Osmond cried. "Maybe we need a little of that enlightened self-interest ourselves!" Although Richard Deacon didn't say anything, he was visibly puffed up with vindication. Hugh gave a long sigh and said, "Maybe we have no choice after all. Let's just not seem *too* greedy when we ask."

Over the next several days, various members of the thirteen fanned out to contact the parties who had shown earlier interest. In addition to Hasbro and Marx toys there were Walt Disney, who had suggested a monumental

Beaverland amusement park, Stan Lee, who had pitched them on a comic book called *The Amazing Beaver-Man*, Hanna-Barbera, who had proposed a cartoon series about the Cleavers with the addition of a snickering dog, and Aaron Copland and Agnes DeMille, who had suggested a self-conscious American ballet to be called *Beaver the Kid.*

The reactions varied greatly but essentially pointed in the same direction. The executives at Hasbro said they couldn't wait to start producing the action figures, but their stockholders insisted they wait until Beaver was back on the air. Louis C. Marx himself said that he was still gung-ho about the idea and would move with alacrity as soon as they caught on with a new network. Walt Disney said with an avuncular smile that the blueprints were all drawn up and that the cornerstone would be laid as soon as the program had found a new home. Stan Lee grinned and expostulated, "Jolly Jack Kirby can't wait to lay out the first issue! Let us merry Marvel marchers know the second you've been renewed! Face front!" Joe Barbera said, "Me and Bill, we're chomping at the bit to hit the drawing board. Mary, Mother of God, we'd start right now if you were guaranteed for a seventh season."

In contrast, Copland and DeMille replied sadly that, as eager as they were to begin work on the ballet, they would be unable to secure funding until the next season of *Leave It to Beaver* was a sure thing.

All the excitement that had filled them just a few days before evaporated. Many more books and scripts flowed in during those days, including Katherine Anne Porter's *Ship of Creeps,* Arthur C. Clarke's *Rendezvous with Rayburn,* and a pair of carefully wrought, if tedious, scholarly homages to nineteenth century authors: Harriet Beecher Stowe, with *Uncle Billy's Cabin*, and Henry James, with *Portrait of an Icky Girl*. But none captured the mood of melancholy and broken dreams as well as the script written in honor of self-pitying Jazz-Age figurehead F. Scott Fitzgerald.

The Great Haskell

by Edmund Wilson in the manner of
F. Scott Fitzgerald

In his blue garden, boys and girls come and go like moths
in letterman sweaters and poodle skirts. Crates of RC Cola
and Nehi Grape march as freshly as troops of the AEF in a
steady procession to his front door, to reemerge in the
purpling garage as melancholy, translucent sentinels
awaiting their surrender for nickel deposits. Wally ushers
Mary Ellen Rogers into this universe of ineffable
gaudiness, this vast, vulgar, and meretricious orgy of crepe
paper, potato chips, and twist records.

Nothing is missing but the great Haskell himself, and in
his absence the stories about him grow in romance. "I heard
he quit high school to make a fortune at a gas station," says
Tooey Brown. "I heard he joined the merchant marines,"
says Julie Foster. "I heard he played halfback for Princeton,
killed a man in the Argonne, bought a movie studio, and
slept with Isadora Duncan one hot, sweet night in Cap
d'Antibes," says Lumpy Rutherford.

"*Eddie Haskell?*" Wally yells in incredulity. "He's just
throwing this party 'cause his parents are out of town and
he's sick of everybody thinking he's a goony loser!"

"Let me tell you about the very goony," intones Beaver, who has tagged along as a cynical observer. "They're different from you and me." But he realizes no one's listening to him and shuts up.

At last Haskell himself enters, wearing an ivory muslin suit and shoes as black as the dark night of the soul, his waves of hair as golden as the waves of wheat in that vast obscurity beyond the city and his ivory grin of self-assurance even ivorier than his suit. "Gee," Mary Ellen says. "He's a dreamboat!" Wally storms out in a sickly green rage. Haskell's self-assurance flits away like a fairy's wing, and he rushes after his friend.

"Show me a dreamboat," Beaver says significantly, "and I'll write you a shipwreck." But he realizes that no one's listening to him and hurries after Haskell and Wally.

Wally in his roadster roars madly through Mayfield, a town of dun-gray tract homes and gunmetal-gray Plymouths and mothers in dove-gray dresses and fathers in flannel suits that range from charcoal to taupe. Haskell roars after him in his parents' yellow car, Mary Ellen beside him. He senses a pair of eyes on him and looks up to see a time-faded billboard where an enigmatic blonde housewife holds endlessly aloft a gigantic bowl of Zesto soup. He shudders.

As they pass the Mayfield Theater they see Wally walking with Marlene, the girl who works in the ticket booth. Marlene is a girl made to be kissed but not to be brought home to the parents, her carmine-rouged and cigarette-draped lower lip a rebuttal to the virginal simplicity of Mary Ellen. Haskell jumps out, calling to Wally, "Come on, Leroy! You've got to give me another chance!"

"There are no second acts at the Mayfield Theater," says Beaver meaningfully. But he realizes not only that no one is listening to him but that Mary Ellen is roaring away in the yellow car, driving right over Marlene in the process.

"Golly, Eddie," Wally says. "You're really in the soup now!" Remembering the billboard, Haskell shudders. He jumps into Wally's roadster and roars after Mary Ellen. Wally bounds onto the running board and Beaver throws himself head first into the rumble seat.

When they reach the indigo emptiness of the Haskell estate, they find the yellow car sitting abandoned and Haskell's father vermillion with rage. "Eddie, it's bad enough that you turn our home into a universe of ineffable gaudiness when your mother and I are out of town," he yells. "But did you have to dent my yellow car?" Haskell opens his mouth to put the blame on Mary Ellen, but Wally leaps in with, "See, Eddie? I told you not to drive over Marlene!" Haskell has only an instant to realize that he's been betrayed before his father grounds him.

In the old man's absence, Haskell is left staring at the wreckage of the party, amid which lies the wreckage of that Platonic conception of himself that he pursued with such faithfulness to the end. "Gosh, Eddie," Wally says, "I'm sorry I had to do that, but…" "Ah, forget it, Gwendolyn," Haskell says, forcing a jaunty grin. "I get it. I wanted everybody to think I was the coolest, but the truth is I'm still just a goon. It'll teach me a valuable lesson to spend the weekend doing chores around the house." Wally watches him walk with lowered head back into the house that now seems carved of ash-gray ashes.

"Haskell came a long way to this blue lawn," Beaver says. "And now he has to mow it." Then he realizes that Wally has driven away without him.

Tag: "Gee, Wally," Beaver says, "it sure is tough for a guy to leave his real origins behind, isn't it?" "Yeah," Wally says. "Especially if he's as goony as Eddie." He turns out the light and through the window, far away, he picks out a green light that beckons him to the orgastic future while Beaver, with a pillow, beats him ceaselessly into his past.

October 1-6, 1963

Again they gathered around the table to plot their next move. Sue Randall, acting as secretary, read the minutes from the previous meeting, but that only depressed them more. Jeri Weil suggested they write to President Kennedy, who had, three months before, promised that before the decade was through the Cleavers would be broadcast to the depths of the oceans, to the outer reaches of the universe, and behind the Iron Curtain. Excited by her idea, they also wrote to the many other prominent figures who had expressed support for their efforts, including the editors of *Time* and *Newsweek*, Pope John XXIII, and Nikita Khrushchev.

Then Hugh tentatively reminded them that some of their most prominent and passionate supporters had been actors who had wanted to usurp their roles. He himself had indignantly turned down Sir Laurence Olivier when he had asked to play Ward. But what if their only hope now lay in getting a major star to agree to join the cast? Clearly, the mood of Randian enlightened self-interest had evaporated, to be replaced by a reluctant realization that any one of them might have to sacrifice his or her beloved role for the greater good of the show.

So they sent telegrams to Olivier, to Sophia Loren, who wanted to portray June, to Marlon Brando, who coveted the role of Eddie, to William Shatner, who wanted to play Wally, and to Charles Nelson Reilly, who had fought to replace Jerry Mathers as the Beaver. In addition to contacting people who had already shown interest, they decided to ask Peter Sellers, who was rumored to be playing multiple roles in Stanley Kubrick's upcoming *Dr. Strangelove*, if he might want to take over both of Richard Deacon's parts (as Fred on *Beaver* and as Mel Cooley in *The Dick Van Dyke Show*), ribald comedienne Totie Fields if she would take over as Mrs. Rayburn, and young guitar whiz Johnny Winter if he would replace little washed-out Stanley Fafara as Whitey Whitney. Lively arguments broke out over whether to recruit Ruby Dee, Cicely Tyson, or Eartha Kitt for the role of the Langleys' Negro maid.

Unfortunately, all of those performers responded that they would love to take on the jobs but that their agents had insisted they couldn't sign a contract until the show had inked a deal for a new season. The gang's disappointment was not unmixed with relief. There was, however, no relief when similar responses were received from the magazine editors, the President, and the Pope. The only one who offered his unqualified support was Nikita Khrushchev, but Hugh, still remembering the terrible days of the blacklist, talked them into not taking him up on his offer.

To make matters even gloomier, fewer literary submissions than usual arrived during those days. No one was able to stir up much enthusiasm for Art Linkletter's *Beavers Say the Darndest Things*, nor for Vance Packard's *The Beaver Seekers*, nor even for the homage to e. e. cummings called *The Enormous Beaver*. But one of them opened their eyes to an exciting new possibility, a script written by the not-yet-hip but already paranoid Philip K. Dick.

Do Beavers Dream of Electric Creeps?
Philip K. Dick

Beaver wakes up one morning and realizes that his nickname is actually an acronym for Brainy Entities Activating Vastly Enlightening References. He also realizes that he's linked to an alien probe orbiting earth, and with that realization mental epiphanies in the form of pink laser beams start popping into his head. He learns that his father Ward is actually a Thing, that Judy Hensler is an incarnation of Holy Wisdom, that Larry Mondello is a Wub from Mars, that Mayfield is an artificial construct, that Miss Landers is in reality a Ganymedean slime mold, and that Eddie Haskell is an alien simulacrum sent to Earth to activate a doomsday bomb.

When Beaver gets to school that day he discovers that where there had once stood a school building, now there's only a hand-lettered sign reading "School Building" nailed to a tree. But when he clenches his eyes shut for a moment and opens them again, he discovers that the school building has rematerialized.

The first person Beaver sees when he enters the school is Larry Mondello. "Hey, Beav," Larry says. "You want to mess around this Saturday?" At first, Beaver is unsure that he does, as the alien probe has informed him that Wubs are capable of possessing humans. But then he realizes that since Larry likes to eat milk and cookies, spit off the Grant Avenue bridge, and goof around as much as he does, life would go on much as before even if Larry did take over his body. Beaver smiles cutely and says, "Sure, Larry."

Beaver has a hard time paying attention in school that day as he can't stop thinking about Miss Landers being a Ganymedean slime mold. But at last he's able to shake off the preoccupation. So what if she's a particularly hideous alien life form, he tells himself. Since she's able to project the image of a pretty young school teacher and rarely sends him to Mrs. Rayburn's office, it doesn't really make any difference.

During recess Beaver sees Judy Hensler and marvels that he never suspected that she was a messiah. Just then Judy catches Beaver staring at her and makes a face at him. Beaver feels reassured that even though Judy might be a divine being, she's still the same icky girl he's always known.

After school Beaver walks past the fire station, but instead of a fire station all he sees is a hand-lettered sign tacked up to a tree that reads, "Fire station." He thinks of clenching his eyes shut, thus making the fire station reappear, but decides against it as he doesn't want to get held up by one of Gus the Fireman's endless stories.

As he walks on he concentrates on shielding his thoughts. He's also learned from the alien probe that policemen can now detect a kid thinking about causing trouble before he's done it and subject him to a lecture for what hasn't happened yet. He looks around for precogs but sees only an uncommon number of Japanese businessmen shopping for antiques.

He walks on to Metzger's Field where Wally and Eddie Haskell are playing a good-natured game of baseball with some other kids. Eddie sees him and says, "Hey, squirt," and Wally says, "Ah, lay off of him, Eddie." For a moment Beaver considers letting Eddie live. Eddie might be a creep, he reasons, but he can't be so big a creep that he would actually blow up the earth, could he? But then, remembering the pink laser beams and their tidings, he picks up a baseball bat and brings it down with all his might on top of Eddie's head.

"Gee, Beav," Wally says. "You're really gonna get it now."

That evening, Ward summons Beaver into his den. Beaver is afraid to go in at first, since he now knows that his father is actually a Thing, but he forces himself to enter. Ward is stern but kindly as he lectures Beaver on the evils of homicide, and Beaver realizes that it doesn't really matter that his father is a Thing. After all, he tells himself, human is as human does.

Suddenly Beaver wakes up in his cryonic tank and realizes the whole thing was just a dream.

Tag: Beaver and Wally lie down in their cryonic tanks. "Gee, Wally," Beaver says, "I sure hope I don't have another goofy dream like I did last night. "Aw, shut up, you goof," Wally says, and hits him with his Wub-fur pillow.

October 6-7, 1963

Joe Connelly recalled, "Me and Bob, we've never been much for reading science fiction. But wowie zowie, we sure did love those old chiller-dillers on the radio!" No sooner had the words left his lips than Barbara remarked, "Say, why couldn't we turn *Leave It to Beaver* into a radio program?" "Neat!" Jeri Weil chirped. "Then I won't have to spend every morning in a make-up chair!"

"I hate to rain on your parade, kids," said Hugh. "But the last original comedy or dramatic programs on network radio were canceled a year ago." "That's even neater!" Jerry Mathers piped in. "They must be really hungry for a new show by now!" When all hope is gone, even the faintest glimmer seems like the greatest opportunity. Tony, Ken, and Frank were dispatched to hit up the radio networks first thing in the morning.

Crushingly, they returned with the word that none of the networks had any interest in new programming, although Tony reported that the receptionist at NBC had suggested pleasantly that they might try some local radio stations. "Oh, come on!" Ken snapped. "For six years our faces have been broadcast from coast to coast, and now we're supposed to settle for just having our voices on the air in Muncie, Indiana?" Tony barked, "Don't be a quitter, Ken! Heck, if we catch on in Muncie, who knows what could happen?"

As they ate a delicious casserole that Sue and Barbara had whipped up, the mail arrived. They found only three scripts that day: Tom Stoppard's *Eddie and Lumpy Are Dead*, an homage to the recently departed Richard Wright called *Native Beaver*, and Charles Schulz's *Happiness Is a Warm Beaver*. Seeing that none of those would adapt well to radio, they began digging through their stockpile of old scripts to find the best one to pitch to their new medium.

They were nearly finished with the delicious Jell-O desserts Sue had made before they finally decided that the devilishly clever wordplay of Russian professor, butterfly enthusiast, and occasional novelist Vladimir Nabokov made his script the perfect choice. It was odd, as Barbara pointed out, that although the script was entitled *Pale Beaver*, suggestive of his most recent novel, *Pale Fire*, the actual storyline was much more reminiscent of his earlier *Lolita*. Little bloodless Stanley Fafara suggested that "Pale Beaver" was in some way an oblique reference to underage sex, but Nabokov's wordplay was so diabolical in its ingenuity that none of them could be sure.

Pale Beaver

Vladimir Nabokov

In Mrs. Rayburn's office sits an anxious Miss Landers Landers. "Beaver Cleaver," she exclaims. "Beaver of my life, cleaver of my loins. Bee-verrr: lips popping open, buck teeth biting down." "Pardon me?" asks Mrs. Rayburn.

Miss Landers Landers reveals that it all began when she realized that Beaver had a crush on her, just like so many other little boys. But Beaver was unlike any other little boy, he was a magical creature, a *rodette*. "A what?" asks Mrs. Rayburn. "Like a rodent, but with a sexy French ending," the teacher says. "I'm brilliant at wordplay." "Could you just tell the story, please?" asks Mrs. Rayburn.

Flashback: the class is on a field trip at Friend's Lake, and Miss Landers Landers can't stop gazing worshipfully at Beaver. Her heart breaks when the families come to pick up the children. But then, getting out of the car, Ward conveniently stumbles, conveniently knocking over June, who conveniently knocks over Wally. With all three of them on the ground, Miss Landers Landers scoops up Beaver and drives away.

"Gosh, Miss Landers Landers!" Beaver gasps. "Does this mean what I think it means?" "The Warden may be

Clever," she says, "the June May March against us, and the brother may Wallow in tears, but let a Cleaver cleave to his teacher." "Huh?" Beaver says.

"Don't you get it?" she says. "I'm giving multilayered meanings to your family's names with clever wordplay." "Sure, Miss Landers Landers," Beaver says, "but…"

"Oh, Beaver, my damnation and my dam builder! You're wasted on Whitey Whitney, that mountain of blankness. Get it? Like Mt. Whitney? And *blanc*, the French for white?" "Okay," Beaver says, "but when…"

"Don't be suspicious of the world, like Leery Del Mondo, or wasting your life in a Violent and Lumpy Rushing Forth. See? That was a play on Violet Rutherford and her…" "I get it," Beaver says, "but when are we gonna…"

"Shall I be more polite and address Gilbert as Master Bates? Or shall I make a fowl insult out of Judy Hen-slur? And as for Richard Rickover…" "Oh, for cripes sake, Miss Landers Landers!" Beaver yells. "When are we gonna get to the *dirty part*?"

With that, she pulls over to a motel. But once alone in the room with Beaver she is so overwhelmed by her pathetic longing that all she can do is kneel before him and worshipfully brush his buck teeth. She falls asleep, dreaming of obsessive poets and epicene professors, desolate European villages and ephemeral Russian butterflies, and when she awakes, Beaver is gone. Mad with grief, she begins to drive, roaming endlessly from Mayfield to Bell Port, over Camelback Cutoff, around Friend's Lake, back through Mayfield and Bell Port and around again, endlessly tormenting herself with ingenious wordplay.

At last it occurs to her to see if he's gone home. Apprehensively, she knocks at the Cleavers' door. Beaver answers it. But time has passed, his head his grown huge, and all the magic is gone.

Back in the present, Mrs. Rayburn scowls fiercely at her. "Can't you see that you did anything wrong here, Miss Landers Landers? Isn't there anything you regret about all this?" Miss Landers Landers looks ashamedly at the floor and says, "Yes. There is one thing. I never could figure out what do to with 'Eddie Haskell.'"

Tag: Beaver jumps into his bed and pulls the covers up to his chin. "Gee, Wally, why do you suppose Miss Landers Landers kidnapped me?" Wally, propped up on one elbow, grins at his brother. "I dunno, Beav. I guess she just wanted to brush your big, hard teeth." He flicks off the light, but Beaver's teeth gleam with a dirty sheen.

October 8-15, 1963

Sadly, Muncie was not interested. Nor were the radio stations of Decatur, Spokane, Albuquerque, Terre Haute, Quincy, Bismarck, Fresno, Indio, Lubbock, Winnemucca, Shreveport, Key West, Biloxi, Nome, North Platte, Laramie, Boise, Macon, Montpelier, or dozens of others.

Ward, ever on the alert for flagging spirits, decided that now was the time to unveil an idea he had been keeping to himself for a while. "You know," he said, vigorously rubbing his hands together, "before I was fortunate enough to join you all in the role of Ward Cleaver, I did have a bit of a career on the big screen." "Sure, Hugh!" squealed Rusty gleefully. "I remember seeing you in *Invasion of the Mole Men*." "Well, that was an amusing little job," Hugh chuckled. "But you know, I did once play opposite Alan Ladd and Veronica Lake." Rusty, Jerry, and Jeri stared at him blankly.

Rushing ahead, Hugh ventured that he might still have enough connections in the studios to open the door to a *Beaver* feature. "That sounds neat, Hugh," said Tony, "but we're used to turning out thirty-nine episodes a year. Wouldn't it be kind of a letdown to spend a whole year making just one story?"

"Beggars can't be choosers, young man," Richard Deacon interjected. "Why, did you hear me saying that when I was offered a role in *Invaders from Mars*? Or *Them*? Or…?" Before he could continue any further with his resumé, Hugh interrupted to point out that if their movie did well at the box office, the networks would be sure to regain interest in the show. "You're right," said Ken. "Look how *From Here to Eternity* inspired *McHale's Navy*!"

Once again the mail only brought three scripts. Both James Hilton's *Goodbye, Mrs. Rayburn* and Oona O'Neill's tribute to her father Eugene, *The Beaver Cometh*, showed movie potential, but the one that seemed most natural for the big screen was by the up-and-coming, weapon-crazy Elmore Leonard.

Beaver is Coming

Elmore Leonard

Beaver, gawky and bucktoothed, his shirt buttoned so tight at the throat that it makes his big head look even bigger, walks right up to Lumpy's gang where they're hanging out at Metzger's Field and says, "You guys beat up Larry Mondello pretty bad. I think it'd be neat to show him you're sorry by giving him a twenty-five-pound turkey." Lumpy, bug-eyed, says, "Has this squirt gone goofy?" His second-in-command, the little one the other gang members call Blanco, says, "Or maybe he's trying to give us the business." Without another glance at Beaver, Lumpy says, "Teach him something."

Blanco grabs Beaver's arms and pins them behind his back. The other kids take turns punching him in the stomach. Beaver doesn't remember passing out.

He comes to on the infield dirt and lies there thinking. A boy can be in two places, he tells himself, and he will be two different boys. There is one Beaver Cleaver. A boy who gets good grades. A boy who obeys his parents. A boy who wears his shirt buttoned to the throat. The other Beaver Cleaver who lives inside Beaver Cleaver had once been the youngest member of the Haskell gang. He had played a big part in running both the Tooey Brown and Chester Anderson gangs clear out of Mayfield. He had learned everything there was to know about a rumble.

The other Beaver Cleaver drags himself home and sneaks into his bedroom. Opening the closet door, he rummages around until he locates the Glatz beste Zwillengabel with the curved, recessed handle, the Milligan Special cast out of aluminum alloy, and the Wham-O Sportsman with the gum rubber flat bands. He shoves them into various pockets and quietly lets himself out.

Beaver rides his bike around until he spots one of the kids from Lumpy's gang. The kid sees Beaver at the same time and a big grin splits his face. Easy pickings, the grin says. But when he comes at Beaver he isn't met by a gawky boy wearing a shirt buttoned to the throat. Well, Beaver's shirt *is* buttoned to the throat, but he doesn't seem so gawky when he whips the Wham-O Sportsman out of his pocket, pulls back on the rubber band, and cuts loose with a steel ball bearing. The kid goes down in a heap, his knee shattered.

Beaver wheels up to the kid and says, "You go back to Lumpy and you deliver a message for me, hear?" Eyes glazed with pain, the kid says, "What message?" and Beaver says, "You tell him Beaver is coming."

"He said *w-what?*" Lumpy sputters. The kid with the shattered knee says, "He said to tell you Beaver is…" "I heard you already!" Lumpy yells. Slack-jawed with outrage, he locks eyes with Blanco and says, "Take some of the boys and go get him. I want to teach that squirt a lesson he'll never forget!"

Beaver, crouched behind the Grant Avenue Bridge, sees four of them emerge from behind the school building. Taking careful aim with the Milligan Special, he lets the load fly. Two seconds later three bicycles lie crumpled in the street, their riders sprawled grotesquely beside them. Blanco is pedaling away from the bridge for all he's worth. Beaver cocks back the Milligan, but decides to let him go and instead spits off the bridge.

Lumpy, looking incredulous, hollers, "Whaddaya mean he took three of the boys out with *one* shot?!" Blanco says, "It had to be with a Milligan Special. You don't hit three kids at six-hundred yards without you use an aluminum alloy." "Who is this squirt?" Lumpy says. "You know," Blanco says. "Beaver Cleaver. Your best friend's kid brother." Lumpy snaps, "Yeah, yeah. I know *who* he is. But what I mean is, who *is* this squirt?"

Beaver counts six of them. Feeling the curved recessed grip of the Glatz beste Zwillengabel in the palm of his hand, and carefully taking into account his elevated position, he takes aim and slings off a shot that shatters Blanco's sternum. He aims again, but just before he cuts loose the remaining four gang members whip their bikes around and speed back the way they'd come, leaving a slack-jawed Lumpy alone in the middle of the street. "Up here," Beaver calls. Lumpy looks up and his eyes goggle as he spots him inside the giant soup bowl. Beaver says, "You ready to talk turkey?"

Tag: Beaver stores the slingshots away and he's his regular self again. When Wally bushwhacks him with a pillow, he never for a moment thinks of shattering his skull with a perfectly aimed ball bearing.

October 15-19, 1963

The cast was overjoyed with the script, and Hugh immediately took it out to try to set up a deal. Sadly, he soon found that all his old contacts were dead.

The older generation nearly lost heart at that point, but the younger set wasn't ready to toss in the towel. As Tony, Frank, Ken, and Jerry played a spirited game of volleyball in the backyard while the rest of the gang looked on, they offered up an exciting new possibility. "How about teen movies?" Tony panted. "That Frankie Avalon is real box office!" Hugh looked up from the steaks he was grilling on the barbecue. "I suppose you're right," he said wistfully. "Maybe it's time that our generation stepped aside to make room for something new."

In a flurry of youthful exuberance, the youngsters tore into the submissions that had arrived recently, looking for the perfect vehicle. Jean Rhys's *After Leaving Mr. Cleaver* didn't quite sound like good teenage fare. Nor did Arthur Miller's *Death of a Man Who Does Some Kind of Office Work*. Rachel Carson's *Silent Pond* caught their eye for a moment, as it showed how the older generation was wrecking the planet, but they couldn't visualize very exciting roles for themselves. But then they came upon melancholic lesbian Patricia Highsmith's tale of obsession, murder, and acne.

The Talented Mr. Lumpy
Patricia Highsmith

Lumpy notices a man following him on the street and ducks into the malt shop. He can't think of anything he's done wrong recently, but he also can't remember the last time a grown-up talked to him who wasn't angry. He becomes terrified when the man sits down at the soda fountain next to him and is already fumbling for an all-purpose excuse when he sees that it's Wally's father.

"Mr. C-C-Cleaver?" he stammers. "My Daddy didn't send you to get me, did he?" "Never mind your 'Daddy,' Lumpy," Ward says. "Sorry. 'Clarence.' I'm asking you to do us a favor. Wally drove our Plymouth up to Friend's Lake this morning and hasn't come home, not even to mow the lawn. We're worried that he's going to miss dinner. We'd like you to go up and talk him into coming back." Lumpy is so relieved that he's not in trouble that he agrees and runs home for his jalopy.

At Friend's Lake, Lumpy finds Wally lounging on the shore with Mary Ellen Rogers, mixing Fizzies and watching the rowboats float lazily by. "Hey Wally," he says, "your dad told me to bring you home." But Wally answers, "Ah,

I'll go home in a couple hours. It's too nice up here. And heck, the lawn doesn't need mowing anyway."

Mary Ellen glares at Lumpy to signal him that it's time to go, but Lumpy only stands there and stares stupidly at them. He's suddenly aware of a brutish hostility for his old friend and scrounges through his memory seeking a reason for it. He remembers the time Wally and Eddy chained his jalopy's axle to a tree, but then he remembers that they convinced him he had it coming to him. No, he realizes slowly. What enrages him about Wally is just the fact that he's Wally. How desperately Lumpy would like to have his friend's easy athleticism, his pug nose, his dreamy smile, his letterman sweater. Not to mention a daddy who lectures him about responsibility when he does something wrong instead of calling him a big, stupid oaf.

Mary Ellen draws Wally aside. "The way he looks at you, Wally" she whispers. "Can't you see what he *is?*" "Well sure!" Wally laughs. "He's a big, dumb goof!" Mary Ellen shakes her head and hisses, "Haven't you ever noticed how he's always following you around and never has a *girlfriend?*" Puzzled, Wally asks, "You mean he's a big, dopey ape?" "No!" snaps Mary Ellen. "Think about that whiney way he talks and how he's always saying 'Daddy' and 'Mommy'? Don't you *get* it?" Wally furrows his brow, straining to understand. "You mean he's a big, goony creep?"

Lumpy catches enough of their conversation to feel a sudden panic. What if Wally tells him to bug off? Where would he be then, without even his vicarious enjoyment of Wally's blessed life? Could he endure a life with no friends except Eddie Haskell? "Hey Wally," he says urgently.

"Daddy wants me home soon. But how about you and me going out in a rowboat first?" Wally shrugs, "Sure, why not?" Mary Ellen flounces angrily off to the ladies' changing room.

As soon as they reach the middle of Friend's Lake, Lumpy beats Wally to death with an oar. Then he rolls his body into the water, but not before peeling off his letterman sweater.

Later, unable to find Wally anywhere, Mary Ellen takes a tentative peek into the men's changing room. To her horror, she finds Lumpy preening before a mirror, pulling Wally's overstretched sweater tight around his massive torso, trying to comb his hair just like Wally, smile dreamily just like Wally, rub his nose with his index finger—just like Wally. Lumpy sees her. He tries to come up with an explanation for what she sees, but he can't dredge anything out of his murky thoughts. Instead, he beats her to death with the mirror and drags her body into the lake.

Ward and June are troubled when their Plymouth drives up to the house but only Lumpy climbs out. "What's happened, Lumpy?" June asks. "Sorry. 'Clarence.'" Lumpy begins, "Gosh, Mr. and Mrs. Cleaver…" But then he forgets what he had planned to say and instead, with a trembling hand, draws an envelope out of the pocket of his too-tight letterman sweater.

Ward tears it open and sees, printed in a clumsy hand: "Dear Mommy and Daddy, I'm real sorry to tell you this, but me and Mary Ellen Rogers are in despair because we're too young to get married, so we made a suicide pact. We're going to go out in the lake and beat each other to death. After we're both dead, I hope you'll take Clarence in just as if he were your own son. Yours truly, Wally Cleaver. PS: Clarence gets to keep my letterman sweater too."

"A suicide pact!" June exclaims. "Oh, Ward, that's terrible!" Ward shakes his head sadly. "These kids today just have no sense of responsibility. Why, where would we be if we hadn't been willing to wait until I'd graduated from State?" Beaver glares at Lumpy suspiciously but says nothing.

"Well," June says, "I suppose the least we can do is grant him his last wish."

Teary-eyed, she takes Lumpy's arm and leads him into the kitchen, where a pot roast is waiting. Lumpy struggles to suppress a sudden exaltation. His lips form the words, "It's mine!"

Tag: Beaver is whacking Lumpy with a pillow, trying to provoke him into a fight. Lumpy snaps, "Get lost, will ya, squirt?" "Ah, come on, Lumpy Dumpy!" Beaver whines. "If you're gonna be my new big brother, you've gotta do this!" "Oh yeah? And what if I don't?" Beaver's eyes narrow. "If you don't, I'm gonna tell mom and dad what *really* happened to Wally at the lake." "Okay, peewee, you win," Lumpy says, and he beats him to death with a pillow.

October 20-25, 1963

The youngsters lost no time in piling into Frank Bank's jalopy and racing off to all the producers of teen movies. But at every production company they heard the same thing: the scuttlebutt among the industry's sharpest trend-watchers was that the youth craze was running its course and the rest of the 1960s would see a return to good, solid, mature entertainment.

While the teen set joined their elders in quiet desperation, Mosher and Connelly began to ask themselves if there could possibly be any other avenues to getting a movie made. Mosher recalled, "Me and Joe, we suddenly remembered that great educational film we made for the US Treasury Department to teach kids how to save their money. Hot ziggity, Washington was always in the market for some good propaganda!"

While the writers sequestered themselves to work on their new script, the other eleven went about their lives. To pass the time, Hugh and Richard practiced their putting in the backyard using Claes Oldenburg's french-fry shaped clubs. The teenagers, still morose from their disappointment, spent the days in Tony's room spinning platters. Little waxen Stanley Fafara took to bed with all seven volumes of Proust's *Remembrance of Things Past*. Sue and Barbara teamed up to prepare a meat loaf, although the result didn't have their usual pizzazz. Jerry and Rusty teased Jeri Weil for being a melancholic lesbian.

During this dolorous period, the gang could no longer pretend that the number of scripts arriving in the mail wasn't dwindling rapidly. One day, the only script to arrive was Mary Chase's play *Beavey*, in which a genial Ward is committed to a mental institution because he claims to be friends with an invisible, six-foot-tall Beaver. The news of *Beaver*'s cancellation had clearly reached even the literary community.

But then, at last, the day came when Bob Mosher and Joe Connelly emerged from their den to present the gang with a script they had written specifically for the United States Office of Civil Defense.

Duck and Cleaver

by Bob Mosher and Joe Connelly for
The United States Office of Civil Defense

Miss Landers is showing her class a film on how to survive the atomic bomb. The film's narrator begins by telling the children to heed loud, ear-piercing sirens, which will herald the imminence of an all-out atomic attack. But, the narrator makes it clear, we can't be sure that there will be time for an early warning to be issued. Therefore, the children must be alert to any searing, blinding flashes of light that fill the entire sky. Furthermore, an all-out attack may come no matter where we are or what we're doing. It might come on a Sunday, a holiday, during vacation, or on any ordinary day—or night—of the year.

As the narrator speaks, Beaver, Larry, Judy, and the rest of the class sit frozen in horror. "Gee, Miss Landers," Beaver whines, "that sounds really creepy!"

But just then, as if in anticipation of Beaver's reaction, cheerful music issues from the speakers and the narrator declares that there's an easy way to survive an atomic attack. All we have to do—the instant a searing, blinding flash of light fills the sky—is to crawl under our desks and cover our heads and necks with our arms. That way, we won't need to worry about getting cut to ribbons by jagged shards of flying glass or incurring hideous radiation burns on our faces.

Now Beaver, Larry, Judy, and the rest of the class sit grinning in relief and confidence.

After school that day, Beaver asks June how best to survive an atomic blast in the house. June cheerfully points out all the various tables in the house and explains that all Beaver has to do in the event of a searing, blinding flash of light is to duck under any one of them and cover his head and neck with his arms. She goes on to say, "I can stop the bleeding from every part of your body except your throat, Beaver, so make sure you cover up! Of course, your hands and arms might incur hideous radiation burns, but they won't necessarily be life threatening." Reassured, Beaver grins broadly.

June has evidently told Ward about Beaver's concerns, because that night at dinner Ward announces that he has a big surprise for the boys. After they finish eating, the family tromps into the backyard where Ward throws open the doors to the basement and reveals that he's had it converted into a bomb shelter. Downstairs, the boys gape at the two sets of bunk beds, the jerry-cans of water, the abundance of neatly stacked food tins, the gas masks, the Geiger counter, the piles of ointments and painkillers, and much more. Looking crestfallen, Wally says, "Gee, dad. How long would we have to be cooped up down here, anyway?" Ward says, "Not more than a week or so, Wally. By then all the radioactivity will have cleared up." Wally smiles in relief and confidence.

But once again it's Beaver who looks worried. He says, "Gee, dad, but wouldn't everything on the surface have been blown to kingdom come? Wouldn't weird weather patterns continue to devastate the planet long after all the bombs have detonated? Wouldn't all the vegetation have withered away? Wouldn't the few animals that survive have gone feral? Wouldn't packs of vicious teenagers prey on the enfeebled survivors? What's the point of surviving an all-out atomic war if the price of our survival is so steep?"

Ward looks stern for a moment, but then his face softens. Shoving his hands into his pockets and rocking back and forth on the balls of his feet, he says, "Sure, it'll be tough, Beaver. But if enough of us don't endure all the ghastly deprivations in order to survive, who would be left to wage the next all-out atomic war against the Reds?"

The entire family grins in relief and confidence.

Tag: Ward has given the boys permission to spend the night in the bomb shelter. Beaver says, "Gee, Wally. It sure is nice not to feel terrified for a change." Wally says, "No kidding, Beav. I'm fed up with diving under the nearest park bench every time the sun peeks out from behind a cloud." But they've absorbed their lessons well. For the first time they can ever remember, they skip their pillow fight and practice ducking and covering under their narrow bunk beds.

October 25-30, 1963

Governments are often criticized for their red tape, but *Leave It to Beaver* had so many fans in Washington DC, from the chief executive down, that Mosher and Connelly's script sailed through official channels with unprecedented speed. Within days it had been approved for production.

The intrepid thirteen threw a party for themselves. Sue and Barbara baked a cake—and not just any cake, but a gigantic cake, because Mosher and Connelly had alerted the show's entire former cast and crew that work was about to begin again and, magnanimously overlooking their mass defection, invited them to the celebration.

The little house in the Valley saw dozens of tearful reunions that night. Cast and crew members hugged each other as if they'd been apart for years. The male crew members were especially eager to hug lovely Sue Randall, even if she was still wearing an apron smudged with cake frosting. The boys flocked around Burt Mustin, he of Gus the Fireman fame, as he regaled them with stories of the good old days in his barbershop quartet. Pamela Baird, who had lit up the screen with her portrayal of Wally's vivacious girlfriend, Mary Ellen Rogers, swapped reminiscences of the show's glory days with Barbara Dodd, who had played a librarian in one episode. Stephen Talbot, who played Gilbert Bates, and Richard Correll, who played Richard Rickover, confessed that for years each had secretly coveted the other's role. Barbara Billingsley and director Norman Tokar lamented the fact that no one had found a phone number for Kim Hamilton, so fondly remembered for her performance as the Langley's Negro maid, in time to invite her to the party. Some of the adults smuggled liquor into the house, which added to the festivities. All were careful, however, that neither the boys nor Hugh Beaumont would discover them.

But in the midst of the revelry, the doorbell rang ominously. At the door stood a grim-faced colonel in uniform who asked for Mosher and Connelly. He had unfortunate news to bring them, he said. In their final security check his superiors had discovered that they could not proceed with the film because, six months prior, little sallow Stanley Fafara had signed an anti-war petition. The room fell terribly silent. In an instant, the celebration had turned to a wake. Joe Connelly remembered, "Me and Bob, we sure did love that little pallid Stanley. But drat it, were we ever peeved with him then."

The guests departed quickly and without a word, leaving only the core thirteen in the silence of the house. But it wasn't to be thirteen for long. Richard Deacon announced that he'd had enough. From now on, he was going to devote himself full time to perfecting his portrayal of Mel Cooley. All stood in silence, watching him walk toward the door. Suddenly, little Jeri Weil, clutching her dolls, ran after him. She was leaving too, she announced tremulously, because she missed her mother.

Shocked and stunned, no one noticed at first that little mealy Stanley Fafara was staring disconsolately at his shoes. As always, it was Hugh Beaumont who rose to the occasion. Putting his arm around the boy's shoulders, he said, "I may not agree with your political views, Stanley, but I will always love you as much as my own boys. I mean, Jerry and Tony."

First thing the next morning, a meeting was called. No former minutes were read this time. As they passed the box of Sugar Frosted Flakes around, they discussed their future prospects, or lack thereof. "Gee," Rusty Stevens whined, "I remember back at the Gomalco commissary we could stuff ourselves on waffles and sausages every morning. Pass the sugar, please." "We took so much for granted back then," said Ken Osmond morosely.

"No kidding," Jerry Mathers piped in. "We even used to have a comic book based on our adventures." "Yeah, I remember that," sighed Tony Dow. "There were six issues. And I was on the cover of four of them." Jerry was about to point out that he'd been on the covers of all six, but a glance from Hugh silenced him.

Sue Randall creased her brow in thought. "If only we could be in a comic book now," she said. "I've heard they can be very educational." Soon the idea began to grow. If the comic book could be started up again, they realized, then interest in the show might be revived. All they had to do was persuade Western Publishing, who had brought out the original comic, to give it another chance.

"As long as it contains only clean and wholesome juvenile entertainment," Hugh insisted. "I don't want to see Wally and the Beaver engaging in any lurid violence like that Mr. Lee was suggesting for his *Amazing Beaver-Man*."

Immediately they began tossing out suggestions as to which script could best be turned into a comic book. Because so few new scripts were arriving, they realized it would have to be one that had been submitted that summer. Eventually they agreed to go with the one written by literary recluse and sourpuss J. D. Salinger, because of his proven appeal to a juvenile readership.

The Beaver in the Rye

J. D. Salinger

Beaver leaves the school library looking troubled. When Miss Landers hands him a note in a sealed envelope to take home to his mother, he looks even more troubled. As soon as she's gone, Whitey Whitney, with that phoney grin of his, tells him that the only reason teachers ever give you a note to take home is if you've been expelled. Beaver calls him a crumby bastard and throws himself at him, but Whitey pins him and gives him a bloody nose. Beaver walks away, because nobody cares where you go when you've been expelled and all.

On the way out of the school, Beaver sees Judy Hensler. He doesn't know why he wants to talk to her, because she's a boring, phoney girl, but the thing about girls is that when you feel crumby you can fall half in love with one for no reason, even the boring, phoney ones, because that's just how it is with girls. But when he says he wants to talk, and she asks why and he says for no reason, she tells him he'd better give her five dollars first, and he calls her a crumby pain in the ass, and she punches him in the stomach.

Beaver looks at the note in his hand but he figures there's no hurry because nobody at home misses you anyway when you've been expelled, so he goes to see Gus the Fireman, because sometimes when you feel crumby you just want to talk to a fireman and all. "Well, Beaver," Gus says slowly, "I don't guess you're the first kid who's ever been disappointed in people." Then he pats Beaver on the head, which Beaver thinks is flitty. In fact not only flitty but crumby, phoney, *and* flitty. So he wanders aimlessly around Mayfield, and through a series of pointless encounters with grownups convinces himself that they're all phoney perverts and crumby bastards, although sometimes they're crumby perverts and phoney bastards.

He decides to run away, maybe to Bell Port, maybe get a job in one of those filling stations where you have to scrub "fuck you" off the walls, but he wants to see his brother for one last time before he goes. He gets a cab home, and all of a sudden he asks the cabbie where the ducks go when Miller's Pond freezes over, because that's how it is with ducks, you all of a sudden ask cabbies about them. "What are you talking about, kid?" the cabbie says. "This is Mayfield. When have you ever seen anything freeze over?" Beaver figures they were crumby ducks anyway.

He knows it'll be easy to sneak into the house to see Wally, because his parents will be gone and the place will be dark and lonely, because parents are a bunch of crumby phonies, always telling you they're going to be there for you when they're not. But when he gets there, the lights are all on, and the air smells like freshly baked cookies, and his mother is at the door, taking his coat with a big smile.

"Come on, Mom," he says. "You don't have to be such a crumby phoney, because we both know when you read this note saying I've been expelled you're gonna put me away somewhere." "Beaver, what on earth put that idea in your head?" June says, giving him a big hug. "No one's going to expel you or put you away! We all want you to feel happy and safe so you can have a wonderful childhood and grow up to have a meaningful life!" All of a sudden Beaver feels the world shift under him. "Honest?" he asks. "Honest," she says. "Now go get some cookies." Smiling, Beaver runs toward the kitchen, but at the door he stops and calls back, "But Mom, if I'm not being expelled, what does the note say?"

June opens it and reads it aloud. "Dear Mrs. Cleaver. Theodore is a wonderful student, but I feel he can use some help with his spelling. I can live with the needless 'e' in 'phoney,' but for goodness sake, can someone *please* convince him that there's no 'b' in 'crummy'?!"

Tag: Beaver sits up in bed, frowning in thought. "Say, Wally," he says in that high-pitched voice. "So does this mean that the world isn't really phoney and kids don't have to lose their innocence and adolescence isn't really a time of alienation and despair?" "Geez, Beav," laughs Wally, "where do you get this crazy junk?" Beaver lies down, still thoughtful, and a moment later says, "You know something, Wally? I think there are some books they just shouldn't let eighth graders read." Wally is about to hit his little brother with a pillow, but not wanting to be rough, he only tousles his hair.

October 31-November 1, 1963

As they all prepared to drive to the Hollywood offices of Western Publishing, little ghostly Stanley Fafara announced that he wasn't going along. Further, he didn't want anything more to do with the show. He had stuck by them through thick and thin, but this was the limit. He would never abase himself by begging for favors from a comic book publisher. They finally convinced him to change his mind by promising that they would lobby to get either Roy Lichtenstein or Mel Ramos to do the art.

They all piled into their cars, six into Hugh's station wagon and five into Frank Bank's jalopy. At Western's headquarters, they were ushered into the office of editor Chase Craig. After they'd made their pitch and showed him the Salinger script, he reached into his file cabinet, pulled out a stack of his company's current comics, spread them on his desk and said, "What do all these have in common?" Jerry Mathers grinned and said, "Heck, Mr. Craig, that's easy! They're all on TV!" "Exactly," Craig said. "Present tense. They're all *on* TV. As in currently."

It was a quiet drive in both cars back to the San Fernando Valley.

So consumed with their efforts had they been that no one had remembered that Halloween fell that very night. They quickly made preparations, glad for the gaiety of the holiday to take their minds off their misery. While the older crowd manned the door and passed out candy to neighborhood children, the youngest members (except for little whitewashed Stanley Fafara, who said he needed to reread Proust's *Sodom and Gomorrah* to make sure he got all the subtleties) went out trick or treating. Along the way they ran into several kids who said, "Hey, weren't you on TV once? We used to watch you a long time ago." The trick or treating ended early that night.

Only one script arrived the next day, and it sat on the living room coffee table for hours before anyone could bear to look at it. It had been sent by renowned English poet and philanderer Ted Hughes, who had discovered it among the effects of his late wife, the cute, blonde symbol of oppressed womanhood Sylvia Plath. Apparently frustrated by her attempts to create a wholesome domestic atmosphere for her own family, she had become obsessed with *Leave It to Beaver* in her final months and had rough-drafted a script for it even before its cancellation had been announced. That script would turn out to have a profound effect on the crusade to bring *Beaver* back to life.

The Beaver Jar

Sylvia Plath

Finished off by Ted Hughes

June has been quietly troubled since coming back home. She enjoyed a weekend of freedom and glamour as one of several Mayfield ladies who won a contest to edit a special edition of the *Bell Port Gazette*'s Sunday fashion section, and ever since she has felt out of step with her normal life of baking cookies and handing the boys their lunches as they run off to school.

She decides to take a night class in creative writing and perhaps write a novel, but the teacher refuses to accept her. "Mrs. Cleaver," he says, "everyone in Mayfield knows what a fine couple of boys you're raising! Why, where would the Mayfield High varsity basketball team be without your Wally playing forward? I can't let you waste an evening every week on a literary pipe dream when you can be at home making sure those boys are properly fed and rested!"

It's not that she feels unhappy, June thinks as she goes through the motions of vacuuming the floors and giving the boys hunks of milk as they barge in after school. It's that she feels nothing. She wonders what real people feel. Then she wonders if real people even exist. Everyone around her looks like such a two-dimensional stereotype. The world seems to be entirely in shades of gray, and she begins to think that even the laughter she hears whenever one of her boys says something cute is only a tape recording played on cue.

At last she tells Ward that her life seems to consist of nothing but minor domestic duties and then long stretches of nothingness. "Well, now," he says with a proud smile, "that just proves I'm doing my job. When I get that promotion I'll buy you one of those automatic dishwashers and you'll have even less to do!"

"But Ward," she says, "my life has no meaning." Ward chuckles, "Oh, June! People in novels have lives full of meaning! But who needs that when life is so comfortable?"

For the next few days June falls completely silent, going about her duties like a ghost. Then one night she blurts at the dinner table, "I'm sorry I've been so quiet and absent. I don't know what's wrong with me." Beaver smiles cutely and says, "Aw, that's ok, mom! We didn't even notice! Did we, Wally?"

The next day she visits the family doctor. She tells him how sometimes she feels as though she's trapped inside a glass beaver and the air is running out. He tells her that there are special hospitals dedicated to helping people with problems just like hers. She asks if he could help her get into one, but he chuckles and shakes his head. "Mrs. Cleaver," he says, "everyone in Mayfield knows what a fine couple of boys you're raising! Why, where would we be without the hijinks of that rascally Beaver to keep us laughing! I can't let you waste a month at a hospital when you can be at home making sure those boys are properly fed and rested!"

June now sees no way out but suicide. She decides to swallow all the pills in her medicine cabinet but doesn't find anything there except Anacin and Bromo-Seltzer. She swims out into Miller's Pond, but the water is so shallow she's unable to drown herself. Finally, she sticks her head in the oven but discovers that she had already filled it with cookies, and they're now just about done. She brings them out and calls to the boys.

She goes back to her domestic duties in a deathly trance. As she is changing the light bulb in a lamp she accidentally puts her finger in the empty socket and receives a sharp shock. Strangely, she feels slightly less miserable. She sticks her finger in the socket again. The second shock makes her feel even better.

Just then Ward comes home. She smiles and tells him she's starting to feel things again. "That's just fine, June," he says as he heads straight for his den. "But now I have work to catch up on." Then he gives her a weary smile and says, "You're just lucky you're not a man."

June puts her finger in the socket again.

Tag: As the boys get ready for bed, Beaver asks, "Hey, Wally, what's 'depression'?" "Ah, we studied that in history class. That was back in the old days when nobody had enough money so they were sore all the time. What do you want to know that for?" "On account of after back-to-school night, Miss Landers told me she was worried that Mom might be in a depression." "That's goofy, Beav! Dad buys Mom all the junk she'll ever need! What's she got to be sore about?" "Yeah, I guess you're right," Beaver says.

When he tries to turn off the light, the lamp shorts out, and the room descends from a palette of washed-out grays to a palette of somewhat dimmer ones.

November 1-10, 1963

Barbara said hollowly, "Well, this certainly does reflect our current mood." "No kidding," Hugh said. "It reminds me of one of those depressing modern plays that are all the rage on Broadway." And suddenly Tony Dow was on his feet yelling. "That's it! We take our act to Broadway!"

Jerry Mathers was trembling with excitement. "Gosh," he said. "First we were willing to be nothing but voices on the radio. Then we were willing to be nothing but pictures in a comic book. But just think! Now we can go back to playing our roles in front of the camera, except for there won't be a camera!" "And if we make a splash on Broadway, we'll have no trouble getting our TV series back," said Sue Randall eagerly. "Look at how *The Country Girl* got made into *Petticoat Junction*!"

Through a series of calls to New York theatrical producers, they learned that getting a play onto the boards of Broadway was no simple process, but that they would have a good chance if they could first attract an audience in a smaller regional theater. So began the calls to theaters all over the nation. The Pasadena Playhouse said no. The Little Theatre in Chicago said no. The Arena Stage in Washington said no. But at last they got a yes, from a nearby but unexpected quarter: a small Negro theater troupe in Watts had an immediate need for a new play. The only catch was that they were only interested in material relevant to racial issues.

Immediately the gang began to rummage through their stacks of scripts looking for anything that would fit the bill. Ultimately they found five to choose from. They promptly rejected Harriet Beecher Stowe's *Uncle Billy's Cabin* because, being a period piece, the costuming would surely be too expensive for a small theater company. They decided against Chinua Achebe's *Beavers Fall Apart* because it turned out to be about Africans instead of Negroes. And clearly Ralph Ellison's *Invisible Beaver* was impractical because, with erstwhile make-up whiz Jack Barron no longer among them, it would be impossible to make Beaver look invisible.

That left them with a difficult choice between James Baldwin's *Go Tell It to the Beaver* and the homage to Richard Wright, *Native Beaver*. Ultimately, it came down to a choice between the homosexual themes in the former and the grisly murder in the latter.

Native Beaver

by Chester Himes in the manner of
Richard Wright

Eddie Haskell bursts into the boys' bedroom and says, "Did you hear that they electrocuted a Negro in Bell Port?" Wally gasps, "The Langleys' Negro maid?" "No," Eddie says, "she's in Mayfield, not Bell Port." Beaver frowns in puzzlement. "Hey Eddie," he asks, "what's a Negro maid, anyway?" "Aw, you know, squirt," Eddie sneers, "a lady who cleans your house."

"We know what a maid is, Eddie," Wally says. "What we want to know is what a Negro is." Eddie looks taken aback. "Gosh, Gertrude. I was hoping you'd know."

The next day at school Beaver asks Larry Mondello if he knows what a Negro is. Larry chews thoughtfully on an apple and says, "Isn't that one of those bikes with the neat handlebars?" Beaver screws up his face and says, "Why would anybody electrocute a bike?" Larry says "Gee, Beav, I dunno."

That day at recess Beaver and Larry, who's munching on another apple, approach Whitey Whitney and ask him if he's ever heard of a Negro. "Sure," Whitey says. "And I sympathize with the Negro, too." "What do you mean, Whitey?" Beaver asks. Whitey says, "If people called you Whitey all your life, you'd know exactly what I mean."

Beaver and Larry, who's chewing on his twelfth apple of the day, are still confused as they walk home from school. They come upon Lumpy Rutherford washing his jalopy. "Hey, Lumpy," Beaver says. "Do you know what a Negro is?" "Why?" says Lumpy tauntingly. "Are you a Negro lover?" Beaver scratches his head through his baseball cap and says, "How can I know if I'm a Negro lover if I don't know what a Negro is?" Lumpy says, "Aw, go peddle your papers somewhere else. And my name is Clarence!"

Larry gets so sick from eating so many apples that Beaver has to sneak him into the Mondello house. No sooner has he helped lower a groaning Larry onto his bed that he hears footsteps outside the door. Knowing that Mrs. Mondello will get mad at Larry if she finds out he's eaten himself sick again, Beaver holds a pillow over his face to drown out the groans. The footsteps fade away, but when Beaver lifts the pillow he realizes that he has accidentally smothered Larry to death.

Panicking, Beaver hauls Larry to the basement and tries to throw his body into the furnace, but his body won't fit through the door. Beaver hacks off Larry's head and now the body fits easily through the aperture. He remembers to throw the head in after it.

The next day word has spread through Mayfield that the Negro in Bell Port was electrocuted for smothering a white girl and stuffing her body into a furnace. Even though Beaver still doesn't know what a Negro is, he realizes that he too could get electrocuted for what he did to Larry, even though Larry isn't a white girl. He decides to flee Mayfield and takes to the rooftops, but soon realizes that the only other city he knows of is Bell Port, the very place where they electrocute Negroes. Which, he begins to suspect, might be some sort of people.

After dinner that night Beaver follows Ward into the den and confesses to having smothered Larry and burned his decapitated body in a furnace. "Well, Beaver," Ward says, "I hope you've learned something from all this." But before he can launch into a lecture, Beaver says, "Gee, Dad. Do you think they'll electrocute me now?" Ward looks confused for a moment, then says, "Of course not, Beaver. They only electrocute Negroes."

Tag: Beaver and Wally climb into their beds and Beaver says, "Hey, Wally. What's the difference between a Negro and a Whitey?" "Gosh, Beav," Wally says, "what a goofy question." He turns off the light but, unexpectedly, the room goes totally black.

November 11-16, 1963

The play opened on November 11th. It closed the same night. After giving the matter much thought, the gang agreed that they had probably not attracted a large enough audience to take it to Broadway yet.

Although they were disappointed by their first venture into the world of the theater, they were still convinced that the stage was their best—if not their only—hope of proving that *Beaver* still had an audience. The kindly ticket seller at the Watts theater asked them if they'd thought of trying to interest any amateur community theaters, and they began to mull over the possibility.

Now it was little whey-faced Stanley Fafara who took the lead. Traditional theater was dead, he insisted. The future lay with the avant-garde. He promptly contacted several prominent experimental theatrical companies, but the results were not what he had hoped. Part of the problem was that he tried to interest them mainly with *Waiting for Wally*, the script that Samuel Beckett had sent them in July, but everyone to whom he read it over the phone agreed that it was by far the worst thing Beckett had ever written. Julian Beck of the Living Theater opined that it sounded like "a parody whipped out by some idiot who hadn't even read Beckett."

The members of the San Francisco Mime Troupe briefly considered an absurdist tribute to Alfred Jarry to be called *King Ubeav*, but ultimately decided that *Leave It to Beaver* was already too absurd for their audience to accept.

Little exsanguinous Stanley's final opportunity appeared when Greenwich Village impresario Howard Solomon said he might consider something "way-out and crazy" for the upcoming opening of his Cafe au Go Go. But the youngster was now despairing of finding the right material. Then something startling occurred—a script arrived. For it had been over a week since the mail had brought any new submissions. At first everyone was excited to think that someone in the literary community might still be writing scripts for them, but then they saw that it had been mailed weeks before from Argentina. It was the work of magical realist and *yerba mate* sipper Jorge Luis Borges.

June of the Forking Paths

Jorge Luis Borges

translated by Pierre Menard

That same placid day that June Evelyn Bronson Cleaver
dies, after a haughty confrontation with her illness during
which she gave or asked no quarter, Borges realizes that the
vast, uncaring universe is already growing away from her.
He wastes no time in catching a steamer to the United
States, and once upon its shores a train to Mayfield. He is
soon being greeted by her two boys and her husband, Ward
Cleaver. After Borges offers his condolences, the trio
excuse themselves to go about some unspecified business.
Borges, left alone, is at last free to study the many
photographs of her that adorn the walls: June Cleaver, in
profile, in color; June playing basketball at boarding
school; June and Ward Cleaver, their arms around each
other's waists, at State College; June, in chiffon and pearls,
stirring something in a pot. June smiling her Mona Lisa
smile in a family portrait in which her husband is grinning
broadly, Wally beaming cutely, and Beaver peeling back
his lips to reveal those Brobdingnagian teeth.

Borges only stays for a brief visit on that occasion, but
in the months to come he finds himself frequently setting

sail for Mayfield and spending a great deal of time with Cleaver. Ward Cleaver is a pink, brown-haired man of hearty mien. He holds some sort of subordinate position in a business firm in the south of the city. His mental activity is pedestrian, cheerful, and faintly juridical. Like June, he has long, beautiful fingers. On his latest visit Borges brings a bottle of domestic brandy, and over his third snifter Cleaver informs him that he has started work on a memoir of his life with June. Upon Borges's urging, Cleaver agrees to read a chapter from the book.

Borges finds nothing memorable about it. Persistence, wholesomeness, and chance have conspired in its composition. His oral expression is overly convivial; his grammatical rigidity prevents him, except on the rare occasion, from capturing the vitality and magnetism that radiated forth in his dead wife's every gesture, her every word.

On what would prove to be his final visit, Borges is greeted at the door by a frantic Cleaver. The house next door to their Pine Street residence has been purchased by a millionaire from Bell Port, and the millionaire, with the weight of City Hall behind him, is pressuring Cleaver to sell his house so that he can combine the property with his own. Dropping his voice, and speaking in that impersonal tone people fall into when they wish to confide something embarrassing, he says that he has to have the house to complete his memoir—because an Aleph is located in the den. An Aleph, he explains, is one of those points in space that contain all points.

Ward Cleaver, Borges reflects, has clearly gone mad. And he realizes that Cleaver's madness fills him with a malign happiness. Hadn't Cleaver stolen June from him? And hadn't he, Borges, always detested him for having done so? But having realized all this, Borges nevertheless allows himself to be led into Cleaver's den and, furthermore, to follow Cleaver's instruction that he must lie prone on the tufted carpet in order to see the Aleph. Ward Cleaver then exits, locking the door behind him.

Borges, fighting a mounting panic over having allowed a madman to lock him in a strange den, sees nothing right away. But soon, under Cleaver's desk, he espies an iridescent sphere that glows with a painful brilliance. Although it is only two or three centimeters in diameter, universal space is contained within it. He sees two gauchos locked in a knife fight on the waterfront of Bell Port, Larry Mondello munching on a raw onion, a library of immeasurable proportions, the Langleys' Negro maid slipping into her bath, every mirror in the world, not one of which holds his reflection. He sees June smiling at him as she poses in a rowboat at Crystal Falls so he can snap her picture, a copy of the first Spanish translation of Virgil, Judy Hensler, in the privacy of her room, gyrating to Chubby Chadwick's *Surf Board Twist*, a letterman sweater, the philosopher's stone, a giant soup bowl. He sees a woman crossing the Grant Avenue Bridge whom he will never forget, Wally battering Beaver with a pillow, a broken labyrinth (it is Metzger's Field), Eddie Haskell ogling a girlie magazine, Che Guevara's beret, Saunders hitting one for the home team. He sees a wagonload of Quakers at Friend's Lake, Miss Landers painting her toenails a lurid ermine, a fist obliterating Whitey Whitney's insufferable smirk, Eva Peron's remains, Lumpy's jalopy,

June's hair in wild disarray on his pillow. He sees the Aleph from everywhere at once and then the Aleph sees his face and he feels dizzy.

"A magnificent spectacle, eh, Borges?"

Ward Cleaver's voice startles him. Instantly, Borges conceives his revenge. In the most kindly way—manifestly pitying and evasive—he thanks Cleaver for his hospitality, and advises him to sell the house. He never once mentions the Aleph, and relishes the look of crushing disappointment on Cleaver's face as he takes his leave.

Tag: Beaver finishes buttoning his pajama top to the throat and climbs under the covers. "Gee, Wally," he says. "I'm sure gonna miss the Aleph when we move into our new house." "No kidding, Beav," Wally says. "It's neat having a point that contains universal space where you can see the whole cosmos from every angle simultaneously and junk." Wally turns off the light, but in a corner of the room an iridescent sphere glows with such brilliance that the room remains painfully lit.

November 16-17, 1963

Although no one else could quite make sense of the script, little achromic Stanley Fafara saw it as the avant-garde godsend he had been looking for. So enthusiastic was he that he had almost sold the rest of the gang on pitching it to the Cafe au Go Go, until Ken Osmond pointed out that no small theater company would ever be able to stage the visions within the Aleph. "So what are we gonna do," he snapped, "have some actor lying prone and goggle-eyed on the stage for forty minutes?" "Precisely!" said Fafara with a wild glint in his eye. Osmond responded with a vulgar noise, and the rest of the cast, although silent, clearly concurred with his sentiments.

That marked the end of *Beaver*'s flirtation with experimental theater, but a new development almost immediately took their minds off it. For days, the others had been making calls to community theaters in an ever-widening gyre from Los Angeles, and at last Barbara had found an amateur theater company in Barstow that would be happy to host them, as long as they could have a play ready in a week.

They spent all night digging through the stacks of scripts they had accumulated in months past, but somehow none of them excited them very much. They were astounded the next morning when, for the second day in a row, a new script arrived in the mail. And this one was not postmarked Argentina. In fact, it had been mailed from Hollywood only the day before. In his cover letter, playwright and famous Alcoholics Anonymous spokesman William Inge explained that he had heard that they were attempting to storm Broadway and, wanting to lend a hand to the cast of his favorite TV show, he had whipped out a script especially to that end.

Come Back, Little Beaver
William Inge

June has slept in again and Ward, wearing a moth-eaten golf sweater and unpressed slacks, makes himself a breakfast of toast and coffee. As he sits at the table June enters wearing a rumpled chiffon kimono over a housedress. "Hi, daddy," she says to Ward. "I had a dream about Little Beaver last night. We'd gone for a walk, and he got away from me somehow, and I couldn't find him again. Do you suppose it means anything?"

Ward says, "Dreams are funny." June says, "Did you remember to say your prayer this morning, daddy? When I think of the way things were when you were boozing..." She shudders. Ward assures her that he did indeed say his prayer, and leaves for work.

As soon as he exits, June goes out on the front porch. With a look of abject longing she calls, "Little Beaver! Come, Little Beaver. Come back, Little Beaver!" But when Little Beaver fails to appear, she slouches back indoors.

June spends the day reading magazines and desultorily attending to her housework. She takes every opportunity to strike up a conversation with whoever chances by. The postman, the milkman, even the boy who lives next door when his ball sails into the Cleaver yard and he clambers over the fence to retrieve it. She wants to tell everybody about the loss of her sons, but Ward has told her again and again that she mustn't give in to her despair, and she repeatedly chokes down the impulse.

When Ward gets home that evening the first thing he notices is that June is still wearing a kimono over a housedress, but he doesn't say anything about it. He good-naturedly wolfs down the overdone meatloaf and the undercooked green beans, remembering the days when June was a wonderful cook, but again he keeps the observation to himself.

After dinner, Ward and June settle down in the living room, Ward with his paper and June with a magazine. June says, "We sure had a good time for a while, didn't we daddy?" Ward says, "Sure we did, baby." June gets a far-away look in her eyes and says, "We sure were the perfect family once, weren't we, daddy?" Ward says, "We've got to forget those things, baby. Things haven't been like that for a long time." Ward soon excuses himself to go to bed, and June goes out on the porch and calls plaintively for Little Beaver.

The next day is Sunday. Ward gets up looking haggard. He finds June in kimono and housedress having a cup of coffee in the kitchen. "What's the matter, daddy?" June asks. Ward can't keep it locked up anymore. "I couldn't sleep," he says. "I just couldn't stop thinking about the boys."

Tears well up in June's eyes. "It's a terrible thing to lose a boy, isn't it, daddy?" "You'd think the least Wally could do is call once in a while," Ward says. "It's not even a long-distance call from State College." With that, he exits.

Hours go by. June is getting frantic. Then her worst fears are realized. Looking into the kitchen cupboard where Ward has kept a quart of whisky ever since he sobered up, she discovers that it's gone. She phones Fred Rutherford, Ward's AA sponsor, but he hasn't seen Ward anywhere.

That evening, June is terrified when she hears the front door open, expecting Ward to be staggering drunk. But he comes walking into the kitchen looking cold sober, his hands thrust into his pockets and a sheepish look on his face. "Sorry for not calling, baby," he says, rocking on the balls of his feet. "But I was feeling so bad about Wally being gone that I just found myself tramping all over town and lost track of the time. Can you ever forgive a sentimental old fool?"

"But d-daddy," June stammers. "What happened to the quart of whisky?" "Oh, that," Ward says. "I finally decided it was time to throw it away." June, sagging with relief, says, "Oh, daddy. I was so afraid you'd threaten me with one of Wally's old baseball bats and they'd have to drag you kicking and screaming to the county hospital again!"

Ward is exhausted from having tramped the streets all day and retires early. June goes out on the porch and cries, "Little Beaver! Come, Little Beaver. Come back, Little Beaver!" Just then a car pulls up and Little Beaver bounds out. "Hi, mom!" he calls. "Hi, Little Beaver," June says. "Did you have a nice weekend at the Mondellos?" Arm in arm, they enter the house.

Tag: Just before going to sleep, Little Beaver looks over at Wally's empty bed and feels sad that he's not there to engage in a pillow fight. But then the door bursts open and Ward and June—he once again in suit and tie, she in a dress and pearls—come bouncing in, each brandishing a pillow. There's such delight in each of their faces as they stage a mock fight, that it's evident the family has successfully surmounted the most harrowing weekend of their lives.

November 17-December 15, 1963

All eleven of them loved the play. Somehow its evocation of pathetic losers looking back hopelessly on happier times seemed to touch their hearts.

The world premiere of *Come Back, Little Beaver* was scheduled for the 24th at the Barstow High School auditorium. The cast drove there to begin rehearsals on November 22nd, only to find that the school, for reasons now forgotten, had closed early. Fortunately, they were able to squeeze in one rehearsal on the following night.

The performance seemed to go smoothly enough, but from about halfway through the play, audience members could be seen straggling out. At the end, the applause was limpid and no one waited at the stage door to shake their hands or ask for their autographs. Afterward, the manager of the Barstow Players apologized and said that they would be unable to continue the play. "I don't mean to be harsh," he said, "but I'm afraid our audience doesn't want to see pathetic losers looking back hopelessly on happier times." Hugh said, "Well, I have to admit, those are some pretty sad characters." The manager looked momentarily confused, but then mumbled, "Characters. Sure." And he hurried off.

Four days later came Thanksgiving. Barbara and Sue could no longer muster the enthusiasm to cook, so they all chose to eat their holiday meal at a Bob's Big Boy in Toluca Lake. They were served by an elderly waitress who, when told that they were the stars of a family situation comedy, persisted in thinking that Hugh and Barbara were Fibber McGee and Molly.

Over the next few weeks, they performed the play in a dinner theater in Bakersfield, an open-air stage in Knott's Berry Farm, a casino in Sparks, Nevada, and an Elks Club in Bishop. Then the offers stopped coming. Following the last performance, when only two people remained in the audience after the first act, one of whom was asleep, everyone realized how pitiful the venture was becoming. Everyone, that is, except for Hugh.

"I finally see the problem," he said on the long drive back along Highway 395. "This play is all about Ward and June, when audiences want to see Jerry Mathers as the Beaver!" Barbara said cautiously, "I'm not sure that's the only problem, Hugh." But he would not be dissuaded. "I'm positive that if we give them a play that's mostly about Beaver, any audience will love it!"

To prove his theory, Hugh needed an audience. For two full days, he holed up in the den of their house, making phone call after phone call. At last, unshaven and haggard— yet ebullient—he emerged and announced to the others that he had not only found a venue for their next play, but that he could guarantee an audience of twelve hundred people. "Where?" Jerry asked eagerly. Hugh paused for dramatic effect, then declared, "Tehachapi women's penitentiary!"

Once again they fell to sifting through their scripts, this time looking for a vehicle that prominently featured Beaver himself. In the end they settled on one that featured more Beaver than any others, the work of world citizen and sex addict Henry Miller.

Tropic of Beaver

Henry Miller

(Beaver speaks to the camera.)

I want to join the human race. No more pretending I don't have testes. No more flogging myself like a demented medieval ascetic when I jack off. I want a body that stinks and shits and stands at attention when a woman walks by.

I want to live in a world that has respect for its animal origins. I want Mom's pot roast to taste a little gamey for a change. I want Wally to stop pretending that the contours between Mary Ellen's legs are as smooth as Barbie's. I want Lumpy to quit agonizing over his flatulence. I want Miss Landers to stop disguising her musk with eau de cologne.

A passacaglia here about women: I don't want a woman who dyes and tints, who nips and tucks and lifts, who is manicured and pedicured, orthodontured and mouthwashed, who depilates and deodorizes and douches. I want a real woman—not my mother.

One time Larry and Whitey and Gilbert and Richard and I were sitting in the cafeteria watching the girls picking daintily at their lunches, and not one of us could dare speak what was on our minds. Were those actual tits budding under pink and lilac and mauve blouses, real beavers hidden under demure, plaid skirts? Or was it all just sugar and spice and everything nice?

I used to think Eddie knew the score. There are some people that you call right off the bat by their first name. Eddie is one of them. There are people to whom you right away feel attracted, not because you like them, but because you detest them.

I remember the night Eddie came to visit Wally, walking with that strut of his, smiling that cat-who-ate-the-canary smile. He claimed to have just gotten laid. But when I asked him to describe the heft of the girl's tits, the aroma of her beaver, the timbre of her moans, he started right away tripping all over his tongue and I knew that he hadn't been any closer to a woman than Mayfield is to Clichy.

To paraphrase Nietzsche: "He who not only comprehends the word Dionysian but also grasps himself in this world, smells the putrefaction." Just so. Proust and Joyce sure grasped themselves, as did Lawrence. Mrs. Rayburn? Not so much. Until we smell the putrefaction we can only deny our animal nature and grow as desiccated and sexless as Whitey Whitney.

I believe one has to pass beyond the sphere and influence of art. In particular the art of the sitcom. To sanitize an animal is to kill it, to consign it, as Dante did, to the vestibule of hell. My father, in his immaculately laundered golf sweater, is the doorman who smilingly takes your coat and ushers you into a realm of sheer antisepsis. Not for him even to know what lies beyond his little vestibule, but only to thrust his hands into the pockets of his crisply ironed slacks and rock on the balls of his feet while his wholesome life remains forever oblivious to the heady wine, the ribald laughter, the carnal realm of cock and beaver and putrefaction.

Tag: Wally can't sleep because Beaver, in the next bed, just won't stop running at the mouth. Finally, he leaps to his feet and smothers his little brother with a pillow.

December 16-20, 1963

Unfortunately, Jerry was unable to conclude his performance because, about halfway through, the audience had to be subdued with tear gas.

For a few days, they could only sit silently around the house, each nursing his or her own private thoughts. Even Hugh could find nothing to say that might rally the troops. Then came one final script. The postmark revealed that it had been mailed in England over two months before. They took turns glancing at a page or two, but no one had the enthusiasm even to keep reading. The only exception was Sue Randall, who read it all the way through and then fell into deep thought. Suddenly she dashed into the den and the rest of them could hear a phone being dialed.

A few minutes later she stepped back out, an almost demented smile on her face, and cried, "Wonderful news, everyone! I've found us another venue!" The others couldn't help leaning forward with a last glimmer of anticipation. "It's the fourth-grade classroom at the St. Gregory Elementary School in Whittier! And as you'll see, it's the perfect setting for this script!"

Then they all began to read the script by car-crazy science fiction deconstructionist J. G. Ballard.

The Beaver Exhibition

J.G. Ballard

Ink Blot Tests. All students at Grant Elementary are required to undergo Rorschach tests. A marked anal fixation in the student body emerges. Forty-nine percent of the blots are identified as "asses," "butts," or "booties." Fourteen percent are perceived as pudenda. Theodore Cleaver sees a butterfly having milk and cookies. A marked preoccupation is also evinced with automobile crashes resulting in torn and mutilated corpses. Larry Mondello identifies his blot as a head-on collision in which Lumpy Rutherford's torso is impaled on his jalopy's steering column. Similarly, Whitey Whitney sees Miss Landers's hymen pierced by a crank shaft.

Apocalyptic Dreams. Several of the students report having nightmares in the days that follow. Students dream of atom bomb blasts, mutilated prepuces, and astronauts in cardiac arrest. In eighty-two percent the cases, the nightmare ends in orgasm. Richard Rickover dreams he is having vaginal intercourse with Fred Rutherford. Whitey Whitney dreams he has stolen his father's car and run down

Miss Landers, impaling her anus on the hood ornament. Both dreams induce orgasm. Theodore Cleaver's dream, in which the Grant Avenue Bridge has been demolished, does not.

The Doors of Perception. The students are then observed to suffer from peculiar hallucinations. Judy Hensler imagines that the telephone pole outside her house is an abandoned rocket gantry. Larry Mondello becomes convinced that his mother's coiffure is actually Gus the Fireman's pubic hair. Theodore Cleaver believes he is playing a game of grab-ass with Larry Mondello, when in reality he's only grabbing his own posterior. Whitey Whitney becomes quite certain that the crook of his elbow is in actuality the crack dividing Miss Landers's buttocks.

Meditations on Mrs. Rayburn's Mouth. Mrs. Rayburn's mouth is variously described as a postulating wound, an anal orifice, and a vagina-like gash. Judy Hensler looks at her mouth and envisions Elizabeth Taylor's shattered windshield. Her teeth remind Theodore Cleaver of teeth. Whitey Whitney sees in her mouth the optimal sex-death of Miss Landers.

Why I Want to Fuck Miss Landers. Students are provided with assembly-kit photographs of various people in sexually suggestive positions and encouraged to mix and match faces to bodies. Gilbert Bates has the Langleys' Negro maid kneeling before John Glenn. Richard Rickover has Wally Schirra ogling a recumbent Eddie Haskell. Theodore Cleaver has Gus the Fireman feeding bananas to a rhesus monkey in a space suit. Whitey Whitney has Ronald Reagan sodomizing Miss Landers on the bonnet of a '58 Plymouth with a crumpled front fender that had once belonged to Yuri Gagarin.

Tag: After their nightly pillow fight, Wally and Beaver get in bed and turn off the light. The room remains strangely luminescent, like the interior of a space capsule. "Hey, Wally," Beaver says. "What's a prepuce, anyway?" "Gee, I'm not sure, Beav," Wally says. "But I think in Hygiene class they said it was part of the pudenda." Satisfied, Beaver re-enters sleep and dreams of the optimal sex-death of rhesus monkeys in space.

December 20, 1963

For several minutes silence hung in the air. It was Ken Osmond who finally spoke. "So this is what we've been reduced to? Do we really believe that performing this... *atrocity* in a classroom is going to bring *Leave It to Beaver* back?"

It was as if a single shudder of realization rolled through everybody in the room. Even Sue Randall clapped her hand to her mouth in a sudden, horrified awareness.

"I'm sorry, friends," Ken continued, rising slowly to his feet, "but this is where I get off." The others watched him gather up his sleeping bag and his bongos and walk toward the door. "It's not that I don't still believe in the Beaver," he said sadly, looking back at them from the doorway. "There just comes a time when a man has to say, 'enough.'"

He stepped out and began to close the door behind him. "Wait just a minute, Ken," said Frank Bank suddenly. Ken paused and looked expectantly at him. Then Frank said, "I'm coming with you."

That shook the room like an earthquake. Next Rusty Stevens began packing up his clothes and apples, then little etiolated Stanley Fafara gathered up his seven volumes of Proust. Sue herself joined the exodus, bursting into tears.

Mosher and Connelly followed them next, ashamed to meet the eyes of their cast members. Mosher recalled, "Me and Joe, we never thought that day would come. But holy smoke..." His voice trailed away, at a loss for words at last.

Finally only the actors who played the Cleavers themselves were left in the room. Barbara, Tony, and Jerry sat still and looked at Hugh questioningly. He looked from one to the next to the next, and then after a long moment he gave a brief nod. As one, they rose and left the house.

Hugh remained behind for a time after their exit. His gaze briefly rested on Dali's wax mustache, on Leroy Nieman's garish montage of Metzger's Field, and on the fringed letterman sweater that Tony had tossed casually over a chair. Then, at last, he sighed and rose. He opened the door, but before he stepped out, he paused and looked back toward the stack of scripts in the middle of the room.

He went through them until he found one that had been on his mind lately. It had arrived during the halcyon days of the summer, when all had seemed bright. It spoke to him of the nature of dreams. And of the dangers inherent in them.

The Secret Life of Beaver Cleaver

by E. B. White in the manner of
James Thurber

Beaver's eyes are turned heavenward, as if he's reciting his poem to the cosmos. Bongos accentuate the cadence of his lines. He's hardly aware of the crowd of cats in goatees and sandals, and chicks in berets and leotards, who sit transfixed by his words. Then a long, passionate sigh catches his attention, and he looks down to see a slim blonde chick gazing at him with parted lips. The naked adoration in her eyes nearly causes him to lose a beat, but the poem is so integral to his psyche that the words flow on like the music of the spheres. Mere earthly passion can wait. The poem finally draws to a close, and the pocketa-pocketa-pocketa of snapping fingers drowns out all other sound. The girl throws herself into his arms, squealing, "You tell 'em, Daddy-O!"

Beaver's father says, "Are you listening to me, Beaver?" "Huh?" says Beaver. He sees his father sitting sternly behind his desk and gapes at him with astonishment, as if he's never seen him before. "Well, as I was saying," Ward goes on, "I don't like the idea of my boy making a spectacle of himself."

...The gang makes quite a spectacle, Beaver thinks, as they come to a screeching stop in the town square in perfect formation. The engines give out a last pocketa-pocketa-pocketa and go quiet. Just then a cute chick walks by and, attracted by Beaver's obvious air of authority, asks, "What are you rebelling against?" Beaver's grin is as lopsided as the rakish motorcycle cap he wears. But before he can even say "Whaddaya got?" a rival motorcycle club comes roaring into the town square. It's led by Eddie Haskell, a former member of Beaver's gang. Without exchanging a word, Eddie and Beaver dismount from their bikes and come to blows. At first each gives as good as he gets, but then Beaver's fists go pocketa-pocketa-pocketa against Eddie's chin and the rival club leader goes down in a heap. The cute chick throws herself into Beaver's arms and gazes up at him adoringly.

Ward's angry gaze is fixed on Beaver. "A boy has a responsibility to fit in with his peers," he says. "If we all wanted to be individuals, how would society function?" Beaver comes to himself in a state of utter confusion. Does his father expect him to answer? Luckily, Ward goes on before Beaver has to commit himself. "Tell me, Beaver, would you want society to grind to a halt?"

...the pocketa-pocketa-pocketa of the train wheels screech to a halt. Beaver, still wearing his Army uniform, makes his way to the rear platform. When he steps outside, the crowd goes wild. People are jammed shoulder to shoulder on either side of the tracks as far as the eye can see. Picking up his guitar, Beaver flings himself into one of his chart-toppers, his hips gyrating wildly. At the end, he mumbles, "Thank you vermuch," and darts back into the car. The train makes three more stops, and Beaver drives three more crowds wild, before they finally arrive in Nashville. The Colonel throws an arm around his shoulders and says, "After the concert tonight, we're recording two new hits tomorrow, and then we're off for Hollywood." Beaver can't help wondering if there's a purpose to it all. Why did God choose him to be Beaver Cleaver?

"Beaver Cleaver!" his father snaps. "What on earth are you so preoccupied about?" Beaver blinks his eyes and mumbles, "I'm just listening to you, Dad." Ward harrumphs and says, "As long as you live under my roof, young man, you'll abide by my rules. And I just won't have a son of mine going to school with his shirttails hanging out."

…Beaver eyes the firing squad. The men look nervous, each no doubt hoping that his rifle is the one with a blank charge. Beaver smiles scornfully. If it was him on the line, he'd demand to have live ammunition. Then, standing erect and proud, and with a faint fleeting smile playing at his lips, he yells, "Ready…aim…FIRE!"

The rifles go pocketa-pocketa-pocketa, and his father is torn apart by a fusillade of bullets.

Tag: The bedsprings go pocketa-pocketa-pocketa as Beaver rides Mary Ellen Rogers. Just then Wally barges in and with a look of utter shock cries out, "Gee Beav, how could you do this to me?" Beaver says, "Well, *you* sure weren't in any hurry to satisfy her needs." Mary Ellen has demurely covered her nudity with a pillow….

A pillow strikes Beaver in the face. He feels disoriented for a moment as he lifts his head from his schoolbook, but then snatches up a pillow of his own, and another good-natured fight is on.

Epilogue

Beaver is lying in bed. Wally, in pajamas, is combing his hair at the mirror. Beaver says, "Hey, Wally, how come they had to name that creepy thing between girls' legs after me? Why couldn't they call it an Eddie?" Wally says, "Aw, don't be such a goof, Beav," and clobbers him with a pillow.

Applause breaks out. Jerry Mathers and Tony Dow turn to face the audience and bow low from the waist.

It was the fifth of May, 1972, the ninth anniversary of the arrival of "Dharma Beaver," the first script to be submitted for the legendary "lost season." For eight years now, the cast of *Leave It to Beaver*—and several of the writers, directors, and other creative personnel—had gotten together on that date to stage performances of three of their favorite scripts from the summer and fall of 1963. This year, before shuddering through the taut suspense of *They Shoot Beaver, Don't They?*, they had laughed along with Neil Simon's *Odd Family* and blushed and giggled at Jean Genet's *Our Beaver of the Flowers*. There was no money to be gained from these performances, no fame, no chance to bring their beloved sitcom back to life; they gathered only to celebrate those halcyon months that none of them would ever forget.

Jerry and Tony belted on robes and stepped into slippers and joined the rest of the revelers at Richard Deacon's massive dining room table. Barbara Billingsley congratulated the boys on their performance and said how she'd always

loved Horace McCoy's script. Hugh Beaumont reminisced
about the years just following the war when he and Horace
had been next-door neighbors and played poker together on
many a Sunday night. Then he said grace, remembering
Madge (Mrs. Mondello) Blake in his prayer, as he had for
the past three years. Richard Deacon waited politely while
Rusty Stevens wiped away his tears, then signaled to the
waiters hovering in the wings. The feast was on.

Through the years the cast members had all gone in
different directions in their lives, until hardly any of them
were even trying to make their livings as actors any more.
But whoever they were in life—policemen, Christmas tree
salesmen, real estate agents, or housewives—they had never
allowed the connections they had forged during those
unforgettable months to slip away. Joe Connelly recalled,
"Me and Bob, we really thought we'd lost something
precious when we walked out of that rented house nine years
before. But begorrah, the best times were just beginning!"

The talk was lively. Already many of them were
arguing about which scripts to perform next year. Others
were reminding each other of the funniest moments from
their failed crusade; when Burt Mustin pantomimed the
rigid colonel from the Office of Civil Defense banging at
their door, his neighbors at the table nearly full to the floor
laughing.

But, of course, it was Hugh who captured the mood of
the gathering best. "You know, it's a funny thing," he said
with a broad grin and an eye-crinkling smile, and at the
sound of his voice everyone else fell silent and listened. "In
all our desperation to keep *Leave It to Beaver* on the air, we
completely lost sight of what really mattered. We didn't

pause to appreciate the great literature we had inspired, for one thing. Oh, sure, these scripts get a bit risqué at times" (which drew a murmur of laughter as the gang remembered the homoerotic hijinks in the Genet script they'd just performed) "but I'm certainly not going to let that stop me from enjoying the fine writing and insights into the human condition that the best of them give us. And let's remember that there's something even more important than great art— and that's people."

Stanley Fafara, not so little as before but still every bit as eggshell-hued, arched an eyebrow but respectfully held his tongue.

"These get-togethers of ours," Hugh continued, "remind us that life isn't about fame and fortune, it's about doing something meaningful with the people we love. Barbara, would you please pass the butter?" And although he hadn't meant it as a toast, everyone at the table raised their glasses and cried, "Hear hear!" Then Sue Randall called, "Time for charades!"

"It has been a lovely evening, hasn't it?" Barbara said wistfully to Hugh as they watched their professional family run laughing and chattering toward the living room. But then a frown crossed her brow, and she added, "It's just too bad that we still haven't found Kim Hamilton's phone number."

If *The Beaver Papers 2* amused you,
be sure not to miss…

Million Dollar Ideas

Will Jacobs & Gerard Jones

It's post-World War II Hollywood, and Ed and Johnny
have proven themselves the fastest rewrite-men in town—
except that they're not content to be doctoring the scripts of
other writers and are burning to sell original screenplays in
which they can showcase their inventive genius. But
there's a catch. Their ideas aren't simply inventive,
they're downright outlandish—not to mention oddly
anachronistic. Who ever heard of making a movie about
homosexual cowboys in 1946? Certainly not the moguls
who run the big studios. Before they know it, Ed and
Johnny have become pariahs.

But will they give up their dreams? Not when a relic
from Hollywood's silent era is looking to make a comeback
and can't find a single respectable screenwriter who'll give
him the time of day. So a partnership is born—one that
throws the past and future together in an unforgettable
brew.

With appearances by Howard Hughes, Betty Grable,
Preston Sturges, Raymond Chandler, Tor Johnson, Philip
K. Dick, Bertolt Brecht, and a cast of thousands.

The Mystery of the Changin' Times

Will Jacobs & Gerard Jones

All readers from 16 to 96 who like lively stories, packed with humor and satire, will want to read the latest book by Jacobs and Jones. Featuring the Sturdy Boys, sons of a famous American detective, it reveals what happens when the times start a-changin' in the mid-1960s and Balmy Bay, the boys' idyllic home, is suddenly invaded by the denizens of a weird new "counterculture."

In seven complete mysteries, all building to a single, startling climax, you will see America's brightest boy detectives try to expose the smuggling operation that they know must lie behind the claims of the weird "Black Panthers" to be "empowering their race"…uncover the foreign mind-control techniques that must be driving a college professor to turn his students against America's heroic efforts to end Communism in Vietnam…and the nefarious scheme that lies behind the sudden desire of young women to discard their foundation garments—and with them fulfilling lives of housewifery.

The Sturdy Boys have helped solve many thrilling cases after school hours and during vacations, but will they stand a chance against the agents of social change?

My Pal Splendid Man

Will Jacobs & Gerard Jones

Will Jones is an aspiring writer with a love of literature who doesn't get out much. Splendid Man is the most powerful being in the universe who has very little time for himself. But when they become pals, Will tutors Splendid Man in the fine arts while Splendid Man helps Will meet girls, introduces him to his costumed colleagues, and takes him on jaunts through space and time.

See what happens when Splendid Man whisks Will off to visit the ancient library of Alexandria...when Will talks Splendid Man out of a profound funk after they see a movie version of his life that portrays him as a dark, modern hero...and when the most powerful teenage girl in the universe develops a crush on our bookish protagonist. Through it all, Splendid Man harbors a deep secret—will his new pal ever learn the truth?

In fifteen interconnected short stories, with humor both affectionate and absurd, Jacobs and Jones portray a collision of the very fantastic and the very ordinary as only they can.

My Tongue Is Quick

Will Jacobs & Gerard Jones

What happens when a two-fisted private eye wades into the brutal jungle of the poetry business? Why do the world's greatest novelists suddenly start writing better fiction when the author of a boys' detective series goes missing? Such are the questions Will Jacobs and Gerard Jones tackle in stories originally published in the *National Lampoon* and collected here for the first time.

Also included are three new adventures of the improbable costars of *My Pal Splendid Man*: Will Jones, an aspiring writer who doesn't get out much, and Splendid Man, the most powerful being in the universe, who helps his pal develop a social life as his pal tutors him about literature.

Finally, Ed and Johnny, heroes of *Million Dollar Ideas*, those indefatigably hustling screenwriters determined to set postwar Hollywood on fire with their highly original—and oddly anachronistic—movie ideas, return for six new stories. Their latest schemes bring them into collision with American icons ranging from William Faulkner to Stepin Fetchit to the Red-baiting agents of the FBI.

The Max Kleinman Reader

Will Jacobs, Gerard Jones & James W. Zook

Max Kleinman is a skid-row genius who from 1946 to 1999 produced 30,000 poems, most of them wrapped around his singular obsessions with fallen nuns, shrapnel wounds, Western philosophy, cheap wine, and All-Star Wrestling.

But does Max Kleinman really exist? Or is he only the twisted invention of maverick scholar Lionel Endenberry? Endenberry claims to have found a shoebox containing all these documents in a garage sale in Van Nuys, California. He exults at having "discovered a soon-to-be notable literary figure," and calls Kleinman a poet of "enormous versatility and vigor." But after months of searching for further evidence of the shadowy genius's existence, he claims to have found not a trace.

The Max Kleinman Reader features the best of those 30,000 poems, along with a cryptic autobiography, a bizarre interview, and a handful of unsettling photographs. But whether any of these answer the questions about Kleinman's existence is a matter best left up to the reader.

The Beaver Papers
Will Jacobs & Gerard Jones

In 1983, the first edition of *The Beaver Papers* chronicled the efforts of the world's literary community to save *Leave It to Beaver*, from the arrival of the first script, *Dharma Beaver* by Jack Kerouac, to the tragic day of cancellation. In 2013, Atomic Drop Press's 30th Anniversary Edition brought it back into print, complete with a new introduction from the authors and a foreword by eccentric scholar Lionel Endenberry.

With such scripts as Tennessee Williams's *Beaver on a Hot Tin Roof*, Yukio Mishima's *The Sound of Beaver*, Jack Webb's *Red Beaver*, and Ernest Hemingway's *A Clean, Well-Lighted Beaver*, as well as such classic homages as Herman Hesse's *Beaverwolf* and Feodor Dostoevsky's *The Brothers Cleaver*, this is the book that launched the careers of Will Jacobs and Gerard Jones…and destroyed once and for all the shadowy border between high art and popular culture.

Printed in the USA
CPSIA information can be obtained
at www.ICGtesting.com
LVHW020238250724
786481LV00022B/277